D1563719

THE RED FLAG MAN
Timeless Dating Advice on Who to Avoid and Why

Brenda Samuel

Book Cover Illustration by Jacob Rosmarin

ISBN: 9798405079493

Brenda Samuel is a writer, journalist, and former international model. Today she lives in Miami with her husband Isaac, and little red poodle, Penelope.

Follow her Red Flag Man Blogs on Tumblr and Blogspot for more timeless dating advice:

redflagman.tumblr.com

theredflagman.blogspot.com

Dedication

This book is dedicated to my dear husband Isaac.

His loving support enabled me to have the fortitude to focus on getting my message out there to all women.

While there are men out there we must learn to avoid, it is important to remember that kind, safe, and wonderful men also exist!

Hold out for your own Mr. Right!

Table of Contents

Forward

Want to get smarter?

Want to marry the right man?

Then you must read the world's best summary of how to do it. The book is called **The Red Flag Man** by Brenda Samuel.

Brenda has fabulous ideas of what NOT to and what TO look for in the right man.

Brenda has a smart analysis about the whole connection that can save you from being in a terrible relationship. It will teach you how to get out of a bad relationship and never duplicate it again.

I am a matchmaker and have been working as a matchmaker for 43 years. I use Brenda's instinct and tactics of how to get rid of red flag men all the time when I talk to my clients about their bad relationships.

This book teaches you the difference between men and women's primary needs.

I plan to save many couples from horrible relationships by telling them to read this book.

Every young woman should read this before attempting their first shot at a serious relationship.

This book makes a very accurate portrait of the differences between men's thinking and needs and women's thinking and needs. It has absolutely changed many of my single's lives and has provided them with more self-awareness.

It's imperative that women of all ages learn to recognize and take seriously the signs of an emotionally detrimental romantic situation.

Tova Weinberg

*FYI, Tova Weinberg is an internationally renowned matchmaker with over 300 marriages to her credit and was recently profiled in the New York Times!

The Red Flag Man

Mission Statement

This book is your new BFF.

From now on, when you have a question or a doubt about the new guy you have just met, or started dating, you will flip through the pages of The Red Flag Man, and see if you find him here.

If you do find him in here, FORGET HIM.

See how simple?

This book is intended to educate women on how to spot the men best avoided.

If we can learn to take the Red Flags seriously, we can surely save ourselves the impending danger, disaster or doom that they serve to warn us of.

The Red Flags are always there.

We dismiss them, ignore them, and gloss over them.

We tell ourselves that our relationship with *him* will be more successful than any other relationship he has had with his past victims.

Together, as a couple, *we* will be so great, that his issues won't be an issue, or, that we can teach our man to overcome his circumstances, personality flaws or deficiencies.

We believe that "with us things will be different", even if all the warning signs are there, and even if it is obvious to those who care about us, that a particular man is not good for us, or maybe even, not good for anyone.

We discount information as "gossip".

We dismiss warnings as the grumblings of a jealous ex, or mean spirited individuals who have a grudge against our happiness, or our heartthrob.

Often the Red Flag man initially exhibits so many wonderful qualities, that we refuse to entertain the possibility that he may be "too good to be true".

We want to latch on to those great qualities and ignore the actual (grim) reality that is flapping in our face.

Too many women have spent days or weeks in their beds sobbing over broken down relationships with guys that they never should have dated in the first place.

Too bad they didn't read this little book first!

My hope is that this book will open the eyes of anyone who reads it and will educate women on how to develop an awareness of the signs and symptoms of the irredeemable
RED FLAG
MAN.

Intro

In a relationship with a Red Flag Man, you may find yourself constantly on the defensive.

Your actions and your motives will be constantly criticized.

"Your skirt is too short, your pants too tight, the soup is too salty, the taste is not right, your friends are dull, your judgment all wrong, your morals are shady, your skirt is too long, your hair should be blonder or longer or cut, stop talking so much I wish you'd shut up."

Both the Borderline Male, and the Narcissist Male personality types, will use criticism to keep you on your toes, striving to please them, and doubting your own self-worth.

Because they need to boost their own fragile egos, they must attempt to destroy yours.
To feel all knowing, important, wise and powerful, they often employ a strategy of putting you down.

If you find that your boyfriend is audacious in his critical comments and corrections of you, know that you are with a Red Flag Man and skedaddle before you spiral downhill emotionally.
The outcome of hanging on to this relationship will be the loss of your self-confidence, no matter how accomplished you may be. You will feel fat even if you are not, dumb even if you are smart, and boring, even though your friends have always enjoyed your company and laughed at your jokes.

So, BEWARE! If little criticisms and negative comments seem to be increasingly creeping into his conversations with you, step back now!

The right guy will make you feel like the most perfect creature in the world.

In my years traveling all over the world as an international fashion model doing photo shoots for magazine covers, ads, billboards and TV commercials, I observed the interactions and flirtations in many different cultures. That is when I started to become aware that relationship issues and "Red Flags" know no borders. Essentially, they will pop up and reveal themselves to us, no matter what part of the world we are in. I learned that no matter where I was, I was able to pick up on important warning signs often just moments after meeting someone.

The warning signs, or Red Flags, cross all cultures because human nature is universal.

The Red Flags are the gifts nature provides us with, to shield our heart, if *only we observe them well and trust our instincts.*
We get into deep trouble when we try to *justify a Red Flag*, or *ignore it*.

So what exactly is a Red Flag in the context of relationships?
It is the sign and/or the information you are given about the nature of a person, or about that person's circumstances.
It is a revelation that the person or their circumstances mean TROUBLE.

The Red Flags are always there! You just have to learn how to interpret them.

I remember a fashion shoot I was sent to do with a photographer in Paris with whom I had a great professional chemistry. He flirted with me outrageously *despite* the fact that he was *married* and his wife, working as his assistant, was right *there on the set*!

He assured me that his was an "open marriage" and that his wife was his understanding "best friend".

Luckily I had the sense to elude his advances as I was already developing some Red Flag sensors.

Often our instinct is to dismiss our own emotional intelligence and to believe that we can change a person with our love. However, that is a false and dangerous assumption. In reality, we will wind up miserable.

It is imperative that women of all ages learn to recognize and take seriously the signs of an emotionally detrimental romantic situation.

As a mother of adult children, some of whose friends are still floundering around in no – go relationships, I am determined to get this important information out to as many women (of all ages) as possible.

There are some wonderful men out there, but we must educate ourselves on what negative signs to look out for, and these signs, or "Red Flags", should be considered **Deal Breakers.**

In particular, certain very common personality disorders may make it extremely difficult to enjoy a healthy, balanced and drama -free relationship. Therefore I provide you an overview of the most common of them, such as Narcissism, Borderline Personality Disorder, Dependent Personality Disorder and Addictive personality, so that you can familiarize yourself with the signs, symptoms, probable causes, and effects of such disorders, as well a projection of how a relationship with an afflicted partner may play out.

You may ask "why can't I just rely on my friends to help me screen the guys I am interested in? Why do I need this book?"

Friends are not the soundest source of advice or feedback when it comes to our men. The reason is that too many external factors come into play when seeking advice from a friend.

The emotional connection with you may cause a friend to downplay an obvious warning sign, or to hope for an unrealistic change in either you or the new BF. Additionally, there may be elements of envy, or even spite, that you are unaware of, in the heart of your friend.

Your friend may be too young and inexperienced to have yet learned the tools needed to evaluate a personality type, or to recognize a Red Flag. Your friend might be older, from another generation, and feel unwilling to label an otherwise obvious Red Flag due to "changing times". (Just know that times change but human nature does not.)

Your friend may herself be involved with a similar man and therefore wrongly encourage you to go down the same path that she did.

Even the best intentioned and dearest friend may not be the most reliable source to help you evaluate the pros and cons of a new relationship. And finally, even if your friend should be enlightened enough to issue you a warning, you may not be open to her advice.

The surest way to protect your heart is to become very familiar with the warning signs.

In short, the decision as to whether or not a man is right for you, is too important to trust to anyone else, but your own, educated self.

My goal is to remove emotion from the equation in the process of evaluating a prospective partner. Let's instead rely on the actual facts to guide us away from the wrong choice, and let's get you educated on how to recognize the right one.

Chapter One

Basic Red Flag Pointers

We will begin with an example of a real life initial contact.

This is part of an actual email received by a single 50 year old mom in NY, on a dating site:

"HI, (no pic attached)
I LOVE YOUR PROFILE. YOU SOUND VERY INTERESTING. THOUGH I DON'T
SHARE YOUR RELIGIOUS CONVICTIONS, I WOULD LOVE TO GET TO KNOW
YOU. I LIVE IN MANCHESTER UK, AM 63 YEARS OLD AND NEVER MARRIED,
THOUGH I WAS ALMOST ENGAGED 4 TIMES."

Can you spot the Red Flags in this email?
If not, you better read this book from cover to cover!

There are 4 RED FLAGS in this little email!

Once you have read this book and mastered the material, you will easily point them out.

Common Red Flags

Any of these factors should steer you clear of Mr. RF:
1. He is MARRIED (DUH)
2. There is a *significant* age difference (like 20 years)
3. Long distance relationship (like another continent)
4. Religious or cultural differences
5. Has reached beyond middle age but never married
6. Not steadily employed or not financially stable
7. Gossip swirling around town about him (may have been marked a "serial dater" or "serial marrier")

8. Substance abuse
9. Uninterested in connecting physically after significant time dating
10. Talks only about *himself* and *his* experiences, goals, interests and achievements, but shows little interest in you and yours (Is emotionally unavailable)
11. Is pushing for too much too soon, too eager to please
12. Seems stuck in his life, can't move forward - Inertia
13. Is cheap
14. Is controlling
15. Displays a temper
16. Has fears of abandonment, is needy
17. Has a quirk or an obsession
18. He is a Mama's Boy

Any of these attributes should cause you to run.

That's right, RUN.

What we want to do here, is to have you develop a keen sense of what constitutes a Red Flag, so that you will be able to discern very quickly, whether a guy is a keeper, or one you should throw back in the pond.
Unfortunately for him, this means that we will not be forgiving of a trait or circumstance that we might have previously thought was harmless, or "no biggie".

Sadly, this tactic will most likely eliminate quite a few men.

One might say to herself, "it seems unfair to fault a man for this or that situation or trait".

Yes it may be true that it is harsh or judgmental, but since we are in the business of protecting your heart we must be very discerning.

The reality is, a **good** man is hard to find.

Let's go through some common scenarios and decide who will not make the cut. And yes, these are all actual scenarios experienced by the women I interviewed for this book.

*You meet on the internet. The date is nice. He is polite and takes you to a nice restaurant.

The next day he unexpectedly shows up at your place with flowers.
The day after that he begins sending you a stream of emails expressing his undying love and commitment.
RED FLAG!
Any guy who comes on too strongly is one to avoid. We want a calm balanced beginning, not a mad rush to the finish line. This approach bespeaks a need to close a deal with someone fast. This man is not to be trusted, most likely has something to hide, and is not interested in developing a healthy relationship. He may be looking to latch on to a woman for stability or financial dependence.

*You are married, but you meet someone who begins to push himself into your life, becomes flirtatious, and eventually tries to wedge himself between you and your spouse.
Though you may have a lot in common, though your marriage may even be rocky and you may be vulnerable to the prospect of a fresh new relationship which you think could be more fulfilling than the one you have with your husband, this man is a RED FLAG MAN. He may be playing out his fantasies with you, enjoying the allure of the *forbidden fruit*, and unable to actually commit to you or anyone else.

He is selfishly pursuing his agenda while disrespecting your boundaries and status as a married woman. The old, uninformed you may have been flattered and attracted, the new you is turned off right away!

HE is married, but seeking out your company on a regular basis, often at first as "just friends".
This common scenario is one to avoid at all costs. You are not in the business of entertaining another woman's bored husband. You most probably have caught his roving eye because he is experiencing a midlife crises and needs reaffirmation that he is still a hot dude, is bored or disenchanted with his wife, is a cheater by nature, or is enchanted with the idea of partaking of a forbidden fruit. (Maybe ALL of the above!)

Whatever his game- plan keep away from this player. Going down this path will lead to heartache, both yours and his wife's.
Neither is acceptable.

*You have been set up by a 3rd party but miss his initial phone call to you. When you return his call, at 2pm on a weekday, he informs you that you just interrupted him as he was in the middle of reading a great book.

Move on now!
This tells us that he is not motivated. He is neither motivated to work to earn a living, nor to work on formulating a new relationship! And, rather than using his time to pursue or review business, he is lazing around reading while the rest of the world is spinning their wheels trying to get ahead! Unless he is retired and comfortably living off of his hard earned successes, move right on past the lazy loafer.

*He is a lawyer, or other professional, and still living in his parent's home.
Forget this guy! We are looking for signs of success and motivation. Moochers move on!
If a man has reached maturity, has gotten a professional degree or a trade and is still living at home, this is a sign that something is not right. A normal healthy male will seek to establish his independence and even to begin to help out his parents and family, not continue to rely on them!
If he is depending on his parents for support, he most likely will try to depend on you as well.

*He takes you on an all -day date, but does not offer you a meal.
Or, wanders off to gaze at the movie poster, just when it's time to pay for the tickets.
This is not just him "being a guy". This is a cheapskate and a thoughtless individual. He wants to enjoy your company while avoiding expense. You are looking for a gallant partner who will be tuned in to your needs and desires and who will be interested in taking care of and nurturing you, just as you want to take care of and nurture him. Ignoring a basic need, or drifting away just when it's time to pay, is a sign of self-absorption and selfishness and may also be a sign of a cheap skate.

*You have heard negative gossip about him from *more than 1 source*.
Don't think he will be different or better for you. He usually IS the bad news you heard about.

*He has reached beyond middle age but never married
If a man has reached beyond middle age (37+) and not yet managed to secure a loving committed relationship, it is unlikely that he will be able to do so once past middle age. He has become set in his ways and will find it difficult and even unappealing to adapt to yours. He may think that he is still looking for his perfect match, but the fact that he has managed to eliminate all prospects for the past 20 years, should tell us that he may be inflexible, selfish, difficult to get along with, withholding, and/ or emotionally unavailable.

Don't pin high hopes on the confirmed bachelor.

*He gets high before, during, and/or after a date
We don't want to be involved with substance abusers. Period.

*He appears to be independent but is connected at the hip to his mom.
When a man feels the need to be in constant contact with his mom, make decisions only after consulting her, and include her in his dates, WATCH OUT! Or, plan to be a threesome from now on!
A healthy person leaves the nest and does not strap it to his back and lug it around everywhere he goes.

You don't' need to allow a guy's mom to involve herself in your romance.

Chapter Two

Red Flag Man Step by Step

Now let's go step by step over each and every one of the most common Red Flags, and give a brief synopsis of how they may manifest:

1. HE IS MARRIED:

Any married man is off limits to us.

Avoid getting too chummy with any married man. Your best friend's husband, your boss, your preacher, your trainer, etc, all may be men that you come into frequent contact with, and who may be especially aware of and sensitive to your issues and needs. Do yourself a big favor. Choose NOT to rationalize a reason to hang out and get too close. It won't end well. Any married man who is using you as filler for his emotional vacuum, is a danger as well. You don't need to risk getting caught up emotionally with some one else's bored husband. So, when his eyes lock with yours across the room, when he begins to move towards you, when he devises an excuse to get together with you, don't even go there!

Step back from the brink.

2. THERE IS A SIGNIFICANT AGE DIFFERENCE

Though a relationship with a significant age difference may very occa-sionally last forever, the chances are great that it won't. From genera-tional differences in ideals and perspectives, to the practical issues of one spouse reaching the senior years well before the other, it is simply too problematic.

Are there exceptions? Yes! Here we are talking about the general case.

Remember, a healthy normal woman in her 40's and 50's often still feels young and sexy. She may develop problems maintaining a physical attraction to a man in his 60s and 70's. She may end up resenting her older spouse, rather than appreciating him.

A woman who is 10 years or more older than her man, may eventually face the risk of him yearning for a younger partner, as he finds that his buddy's partners are all either close to their own age or even 20 years younger.

In 15 or 20 years, will he look at her and feel that he got gypped of an age appropriate younger partner?
Or, worst of all, will he stray, and break her heart?

3. LONG DISTANCE RELATIONSHIP
Trying to forge a long lasting committed relationship from a great distance is a recipe for failure.

We need the frequent and casual contact that a logistically desirable relationship offers. It really is the only way to get a fully faceted picture of the emotional make up and the real life circumstances of a person. We don't want to risk only seeing his best self.

In a long distance relationship the individuals involved get to project and to reveal only those aspects that they wish to reveal. They can actively edit your exposure to the actual reality they are living. We need the nitty gritty facts only available to us when he is on the scene on a daily, or at least weekly, basis.

It is not realistic to conduct a romantic flirtation on line, or long distance, and then expect not to be scammed, surprised and disappointed when you finally meet in person. The small hints we garner from daily contact, will not be apparent to us from afar.

Additionally, there is a lot of pressure on a couple when they are finally able to be reunited for a limited amount of time. Expectations are more pronounced and disappointments more profoundly felt as the clock ticks on toward their next inevitable separation.

The normal highs and lows of a typical romance are exaggerated into great dramas when the two of you only have a few days together at a time.

He wants to go into his Man Cave and chill a bit?
You feel rejected and insecure.
You want to go dancing, biking, dining out, etc?
He feels the pressure when all he wants to do is veg in front of the TV with a slice of pizza.

It's a difficult balancing act fraught with expectations and disappointments that can often sabotage the relationship.

Then of course there is the worst case but not uncommon scenario where he has actually got another woman in his life that he has kept secret from you!

4. RELIGIOUS/CULTURAL DIFFERENCES
Often a commitment phobic person will be inclined to pursue a partner of a different culture or religion, (or any other impossible situation), because of a subconscious need for built- in relationship busters.
He can always pull out the religious or cultural differences card, if need be, and use it as a handy little tool to pull the plug on the relationship, if and when it nears the commitment mark.

So, what I am telling you here is that you may have to deal not only with the obvious and inherent difficulties of cultural or religious differences, but that you may well be confronting a commitment phobic individual who is actually attracted to you because of them!

Even if you should marry, cultural and religious differences are a well known recipe for stress, as you struggle to sort out whose customs, holidays and beliefs should be followed in your home.

To be safe, pick someone with similar values.

5. Has Reached Beyond Middle Age but Never Married
Do not hold high hopes that you will succeed in snagging that confirmed bachelor you have your eye on. If he has not managed to secure a committed relationship by the age of 50, he is not a safe bet. He most probably is commitment phobic or emotionally unavailable. He may lead you on, telling you that he has never met the "right girl"; however, it should be clear to you that she does not exist. This can be a very frustrating and disappointing relationship, if you are hoping for marriage. Consider this a big Red Flag and move on.

6. Not Steadily Employed
You do NOT want this one!
 Any responsible adult male will have seen to it that he has a steady income source before he embarks on a serious relationship, unless he is a Gigolo whose career objective is to escort wealthy women around town and provide sexual favors in return for her financial favors.

Do not date a man who does not have a steady income unless you are cool with winding up being the bread winner in your relationship and marriage. Do not make excuses for his lack of employment, or financial resources, and do not assure yourself that it is only temporary or that he is just experiencing a bad patch.

A mature man without an income source is a Major in the Red Flag Army!

7. Gossip Swirling around Town about Him
How often do we hear gossip about a man, and choose to ignore it and date him anyway?
My feeling is that if people (more than 1 person) are talking about him negatively, he is a Red Flag Man. Better not to risk involvement with him, then to get hurt by him. If you hear that he has cheated on a wife or girlfriend, is a serial dater or serial marrier, a drunk, a drug user, gay posing as straight, has a temper, is looking for a woman with money, etc... any negatives at all, don't bank on being the one to change or improve him.

Remember the old adage "where there's smoke, there's fire" and run the other way to avoid getting burnt.

8. Talks only about himself and his achievements, shows little interest in you and yours
What a bore!
Who wants to listen to him blabber on, bragging about himself or sharing his war stories from his failed relationships?
Showing an interest in the *other person* is a very important and telling facet of a personality. It bespeaks a desire to connect with someone emotionally. We are seeking interest and empathy from an emotionally available partner. If it's all about him, he is probably a narcissist. FORGET him.

9. Is Pushing for Too Much Too Soon, Is Too Eager to Please
A healthy relationship is one that evolves over time and allows both parties to learn about each other, develop a history and grow together. When a man is smothering you with calls, texts, plans and gifts very early on, and pressuring you to take the relationship to the next level before you are comfortable doing so, he is a Red Flag Man.
He may have something to hide. He may be controlling. He may need to rope you in before you gain awareness of his undesirable issues.

10. Is Cheap
Yuk!! It is highly undesirable to be with a cheap person.

If he is withholding emotionally or financially he is a Red Flag Man and we don't want him.

A desirable partner is one who is generous! He should want to show you signs of his affection and he should want to give you tokens of his affection.

He should be paying for your dates, bringing you little gifts now and then such as flowers, cards, chocolates, etc. If you mention a perfume you love, or a book you are planning to read, it is a great sign of thoughtfulness and generosity if he surprises you with these things. It is also important that he gives you a decent and appropriate birthday and Xmas gift.

If money is an issue for him, he can be generous with his words, time and gestures. Even a single rose, or a photo of the two of you framed nicely, is giving and thoughtful. If after dating him for a few months, there are no signs that his heart and wallet are open, close the door on him.

11. Is Controlling
Does he have to run the show? Does he try to dictate what you wear, where you go, what you order from the menu, who you socialize with and who you must avoid? Does he try to isolate you from those who care about you? Does he stalk your social media? Is he critical of you? Is he a fault finder? These are very dangerous signs in any person, and can be very damaging to a woman's self-esteem.
If he is showing signs of controlling behavior in the dating stage, know that this is just a preview of major marriage misery! Unless you are prepared to be a door mat, DROP the control freak.

12. He has a bad Temper
Does he snarl under his breath at the waiter? Does he exhibit signs of road rage? Does he get snippy with you when you disagree? Is he easily riled up? If yes to any of these, he may have anger management issues or be a misogynist, Bi Polar, or Borderline.
Do not delude yourself into thinking that he will protect you from his temper. In fact, the more comfortable he becomes with you, the more easily he will unleash it on you.

13. Has Fears of Abandonment, is Needy

A man with a history of being abandoned either in childhood or in a previous relationship may harbor abandonment fears. These fears can seriously impact his ability to forge a healthy trusting bond. It can be very frustrating to be with someone who cannot trust, and who is always on the lookout for signs of rejection.

Unless he goes for therapy, you may have to give up on a man who expresses distrust of people in general, or who reads rejection into innocent remarks or oversights. Until he gets help to gain perspective on his issues, this relationship could prove to be an uphill battle in an endless war.

14. Seems Stuck, can't Move Forward

A normal healthy individual wants to grow and evolve. Seeking new experiences and achieving goals are fundamental aspects of life, both in and outside of a relationship.

A man must exhibit the desire to grow the relationship to the next level of trust and commitment.
This may be by taking a class together, traveling together, bringing you to meet his friends and family, going to couples therapy if necessary, expressing the desire to be exclusive, and talking about a future together.
 If he is mired in inertia, unable or unwilling to do this, then he is a Red Flag Man.

15. Substance Abuse

A substance abuser is incapable of offering a healthy stable relationship and must be avoided. Any indication of drug use or too much alcohol use, etc., is a Red Flag.
Often the user is using to buffer himself from emotions in general. That buffer is a barrier as far as you are concerned. We want a mate who embraces life, not shields himself from it by drinking or drugging his way into emotional oblivion.

Some very real problems in a relationship with a substance abuser include:
Neglect
Dramatic mood swings and paranoia
Irrational anger
Physical violence
Verbal assaults

Domestic violence
Financial hardship
Criminality
Children who grow up believing that substance abuse is normal behavior
Infidelity
Sexual assaults
Traumatized children

Enough said?

Don't justify his usage; just remove yourself from the equation.

16. Uninterested to connect physically
Not all men are sexual beings driven by desire. We do occasionally encounter the A-Sexual male, often appearing in the guise of polite respectability or religious observance. It can be confusing and negatively impact the self-esteem of a woman interested in progressing in her relationship, if she comes up against this barrier.
Unless a man is on the religious level of a priest or monk, he should be exhibiting a healthy motivation to get to 1st base pretty quickly, with the objective being the home run.
If he shies away from loving intimate contact with you, run.

17. Has a quirk or strange Obsession
A grown man who still needs his "blankie"?
You can't make this stuff up!

In a real- life case I know of, a single, attractive young physician admitted to wearing his baby blanket around his neck and shoulders whenever he felt ill or stressed out.
He also kept a tank of turtles in his bedroom which stank up the place.

I can't help but feel that the turtles represented the fellow himself, seeking emotional shelter under a fuzzy shell.

A middle aged executive obsessed with anything Disney, sporting Mickey Mouse cuff links, dated a friend of mine. His home featured Mickey Mouse art, mugs, etc. He wore knit polo shirts with a mouse logo and fantasized about getting married... guess where... and all the while, he was also addicted to porn, spending long hours indulging on line!

Hobbies and collections of memorabilia are acceptable, of course, but please steer clear of anyone who exhibits an unnatural fixation on anything.

Balanced and **well-adjusted** are the descriptions we are looking for.

Now, what if you are dating a guy and have not picked up on any of the above situations yet?
What if all is going along smoothly until... it isn't?!
What if he begins to "change"?

Has your boyfriend suddenly disappeared like a poof of smoke?
No more texts coming in from him?
Is he not calling you, returning your calls or texting you back?

Are you confused or even worried, because you two have NOT broken up, yet he is not communicating with you?

Welcome to THE SILENT TREATMENT!
This is a nifty little method which some people utilize to avoid dealing with an uncomfortable or inconvenient issue which has surfaced.

It doesn't mean that he has left you.
He is not necessarily *gone for good*; he is simply using this tactic to gain control and distance.

Your boyfriend either doesn't want to deal with a subject you have brought up, an argument that is awaiting resolution, a topic that needs addressing but may be stressful, or a commitment that you need from him.

He also may be using the silent treatment to punish you for a "transgression" he feels you have committed against him.

Your boyfriend quite possibly may be using the space he has created to go out there and check out his options.

THE SILENT TREATMENT - How convenient!

An additional benefit to him is that the silent treatment throws you off balance, makes you squirm, makes you miss him and with any luck, may even put you into the mindset that *any* contact from him, after a dry spell like this, is preferable than this torture, ensuring you will be sure to be on your "best behavior "in order to prevent the possibility of him going missing again! (Oh boy! He is in control now!)

A healthy normal male will never ever employ this tactic.
He loves his lady and *prefers to establish a sense of harmony and safety in the relationship*.

A healthy male partner encourages his lady to tell him what is bothering her. He is working toward, not running away from commitment. If he offended or upset her he seeks to right the wrong, not to disappear for days at a time. If she offended or upset him, he is capable of expressing his upset in a non confrontational way, and he has no need to "punish" her.

Be aware that the disappearing act is NOT normal acceptable behavior in a relationship and is not to be tolerated. The one thing we don't want to do is to accept such behavior and allow unhealthy patterns to form.

So what to do if your guy has disappeared for a while and then resurfaces as if nothing has happened?

I suggest meeting with him in person and explaining to him that you are more than willing to communicate about whatever is bothering him, but that you are not prepared to be in a relationship with a partner who thinks it is acceptable to cut off communication with you.

If he is not cool with that, skedaddle! Your man is a Red Flag Man.

Chapter Three

Married Red Flag Man –
The Unavailable Player

This suave handsome creature will unabashedly move in on his prey with no qualms whatsoever, despite the fact that he is not available for a relationship. He is a married man.

He is successful, self-confident and a mover / shaker.

He moves in the highest echelons of society.

Because of his cocky self-confidence and success, he feels that he is entitled to whatever he wants, whenever he wants it, and like a kid in the candy store, he goes after it.

He will make his initial moves via friendship, using a platonic platform to gain access to your heart, and with any luck, your bed.

You most probably already share a bond of sorts in the social circles you both move in, so "player man" will try to utilize that to entice you into a rendezvous.

Soon enough he will be unburdening his tortured soul, almost as fast as he unbuttons your blouse.

You may find yourself being drawn in by his charms, achievements and vulnerabilities.

But honey, remember this, you are his game and he is on the hunt.

Bored and frustrated with his home life, and feeling entitled to fun and excitement, he moves in for the kill when he encounters an attractive woman. (Even better if she too is unavailable!).

This guy has nothing to offer, as what he has belongs to his wife and kids. What he wants is a sexy challenge. He may entice you to spend "innocent "time with him, by inviting you to accompany him to parties, cultural events, and dinners out... Eventually he will suggest staying in and ordering take – out, (when the wife is not around) because he is "lonely", "bored", "feeling down", whatever, and then....then watch out!

This seasoned charmer will play your heart like a violin as he lures you into his lair. Once your sympathies for him are engaged, it is hard to disengage.

With flattery and passion he will make you believe that you just may be the woman who can fix his empty disappointing personal life.
Warning! The moment you start to believe this falsehood, and start to develop real feelings and hopes for a future with him, his desire to keep up the charade will go cold.

He wants only fun and games with you silly! You were his latest challenge, nothing more.

How does he manifest the sudden game change?

He calls you less frequently. He shows small signs of disrespect towards you such as being on the phone when you arrive for a date at the appointed time, or not offering to buy you dinner, a drink, or even a glass of water, (though you made plans for a dinner-time get together).
He may start to express appreciation for other women, in your presence....

Though all married men are off limits to you, this type is particularly insidious because he glides in on the friendship platform and then uses it to tempt and lure you into more. The trust you already have in him as a friend, is what trips you up as you begin to go to the next level and then the next... after all, he wouldn't scam you, his friend, would he?
Yep! He will also lure in his female shrink, his next door neighbor and his rabbi's wife if he has the chance!

This personality type is a bit of a sexual predator, or sex addict. . He is easily bored, and almost like a bucket with a hole in it, he can never be filled up, or satiated. His fulfillment comes from the hunt.
Once he has snagged his prey, he needs to move on to the next kill.

This personality type is not sensitive to the needs and feelings of another. He is self-absorbed, controlling, and needy. He has no desire to give to another person, only to use them for his own gratification. He resents the responsibilities he has towards his family, and really wants nothing more than to play and have fun whenever possible. Because he is in a position of power and responsibility he feels that he has paid his dues to society and that he is owed a good time.

How did he get like this?
Perhaps he had been given too much responsibility at an early age.
He was always good at what he did and was intermittently shown a lot of appreciation for his achievements. At other times he was probably under appreciated. He learned to feel unfulfilled by his achievements.
He may have experienced abandonment or rejection from his parents in early childhood, which later set him up to grab life's goodies because who knew if or when he would have the opportunity to get them again? Therefore he is missing the chip that makes one trusting, reliable and honorable, due to a lack of early life emotional support.

His parents may have taught him a sense of entitlement to life's goodies.
Maybe he experienced a tragedy in his youth, which caused him to develop the desire to grab happiness wherever and whenever the opportunity arises.
He may have married and started a family very early in life, and little by little began to feel that there must be more gratification out there just waiting for him. It can be all of the above or something else entirely!

How to recognize him:
First of all he is MARRIED.
Stay away
He is a friend, and yet is flirting with you
He wants to spend alone time with you and tell you about his private, personal pain
In short, *everything is inappropriate*, so you don't need to be there

Chapter Four

Married Man Seeking Upgrade

It is possible to wind up involved with a married man who, upon first glance, did not appear to be on the prowl.

Picture this:
A very nice, respected, established, successful and devoted husband/father somehow stumbles onto your path.
He is involved with all kinds of charities, a leader in his community with impeccable credentials and reputation. You meet socially, no flirting at all at first, and he is very open and up front about the fact that he is a married man, committed to staying married.

Somehow though, he enjoys talking to you so much, has so many good laughs with you, and you both relate so well to one another, that a little spark of chemistry gets going.

One minute you are commiserating over some shared mishap, misery or interest, and the next moment, KABOOM! A fire is lit in the parched earth of his heart, and yours!

Even the most cautious, conservative and upright woman could accidentally get caught up with a married man, who on a subconscious level, is seeking an upgrade.

Your conversations are compelling and so the two of you start to look forward to communicating as often as possible. You may find yourselves texting throughout the day... Always on the up and up, no improprieties here... But then, over time, the both of you sort of become a bit "addicted" to these conversations... and eventually, yearn to spend some quality time together.

So perhaps you meet to take in a movie, a concert, or go for an innocent walk together…. And then, the next thing you know, the both of you are fantasizing about MORE.

He may become overtly flirtatious and start to put the moves on you.
You may hold back at first.
You may even send him off for a good dose of therapy, even marital counseling.
Though you find him attractive and wish that he were yours, you are a good girl and don't wish to be the source of another woman's heartache… therefore you remain held back physically and emotionally.
But eventually, he just wears you down. He may begin to insist that his marriage isn't so rock solid or gratifying after all, and having you in his life has opened his eyes to the possibilities of what might have been, or better yet, what could be.

He speaks to you of the traveling he would love to do with you, the sights the both of you could see and appreciate and the heights that the two of you can reach, if only you were together.
Perhaps you could run off and get married in Venice?
Soon enough your heart begins to melt. Plus you feel sorry for the poor fellow who ended up with the wrong wife. Why shouldn't it have been you?

You pity yourself… can you really let the man of your dreams slip out of your fingers only to return to his unfulfilling life with his dull wife?
Why shouldn't you both now pursue the possibility of a romantic happy ending together? Doesn't everybody deserve a shot at happiness??

Your credit card bills escalate as your shopping trips have become focused on pleasing the upgrade -seeker.
At this point there is no more denying the truth. You two are stuck on each other and frantically trying to figure out where to go from here, and how to avoid hurting the poor unsuspecting wife.

He visits a divorce lawyer and gets a handle on what he can expect the financial impact to be, should he decide to make the leap.

You may decide to try to separate for a while; just to make sure that this is the "real deal" before any drastic action is taken.
But the separation is torture!! Neither one of you can bear it!

And so you begin the planning stage.

He will just get through the upcoming holidays, and then he will drop the bomb on her.
"Maybe she shouldn't know there is another woman", you suggest... "Just let her think that you are unhappy and want out" – this sounds good to him, and the strategy is finalized.

At this point you are all in. You have caved to the "reality" that he wants a life with you and that in fact, he cannot face a life without you.
It's not your fault. You never set out to hurt anyone, and certainly never anticipated this!
But here it is, so you may as well make the best of it.
It must have been fate.

Next the upgrade seeker prepares and perfects the speech he will spring on his wife, when the time is right... and then... **It's time**.

You are waiting by the phone because when it rings, it will be him, a FREE man, on his way into your loving arms at last.

Yours, all yours.

Finally the phone call comes!
His voice quivers as he relates to you how difficult the conversation was. In fact, it was the most difficult conversation he has ever had in his life!
She cried. She promised to do anything, change anything, to make him happy, and to make him stay.
What's a nice guy to do?
He simply cannot inflict this pain on his innocent wife of 25 years.
After all, what was her crime?
Nope, "sorry," he tells you, but he had better get to work on the marriage.

A week later, an email from him
"The marriage counseling is proving helpful and the future is looking promising. Good luck to you and goodbye."

What??? What just happened??
How did it go from "I can't live without you" to "we are working on our marriage and it looks promising"?

You take to your bed for a few days and cry your eyes out, all the while chastising yourself for going down the fool's path.

Yes he is a good guy. He *was* tempted to start afresh, with you, but he is too damn nice to pull it off.

This can and does happen!

How to recognize a guy like him?
He is married, respectable, and his marriage is intact.
He seeks out contact with an attractive single woman, and allows it get too intense.
That's enough... back off right here and now
This guy isn't going anywhere. He is just playing out his fantasies of what might have been, at the expense of your broken heart.

No matter what he pledges and how deeply he may even believe it, deep inside he knows he is a good guy and he cannot go down the path of the cheater. He has just tried it on for size.

How did he become the upgrade- seeking -almost -cheater?
He probably married and started his family very young in life. He achieved success on every level. He became a respected member, even a leader, in his community.
His wife most likely stayed home to care for the children and household, and did not have the time or inclination to be much involved in affairs outside the home.
At a certain point he noticed that his wife is a bit plain. Maybe she put on a few extra pounds over the years. She is not the most titillating of conversationalists.
He can't help but begin to notice other woman...
He is deserving of a bright, beautiful partner after all, isn't he?
However, his parents raised him right.
He was always a good boy who went out of his way to please them.
Perhaps they were holocaust survivors, or struggled financially, in which case he has always felt responsible and over protective of them.

So when push comes to shove, this Eagle Scout will do no wrong, because he is programmed to protect and preserve his family.

Our Married Man-Seeking Upgrade possesses classic narcissistic tendencies but is controlled by his conscience.

Of course, he only begins to confront his conflicts with the Greater Good, after he has taken you on the emotional roller coaster ride of your life.

You have soared to the highest peaks of excitement with your perfect ideal of a partner, once he awoke from his slumber to cast you in the role of his ideal match. But then you plummeted to despair as his conscience prodded him back to the reality that he can do no wrong.

Stay out of his path.

He is going to stick with his status quo and he will not pay the price of the upgrade.

Chapter Five

Red Flag Man - The Unattainable Dream Boat

This guy represents what every woman thinks she wants.

He is tall and handsome. He dresses well. He has a worldly sophistication, is educated and successful. What more do you need?

The first date is often a bit like an interview, with him sussing you out, making sure that you meet his requirements of look, personality and demeanor. If you do meet the above set of criteria, the dreamboat will go into high gear and the pursuit begins!

Suddenly, he can't see you often enough... Calls and texts come frequently.

The first few dates can feel magical with both of you (seemingly) feeling that the other is that long lost other half they have been searching their whole life for!
Wow!! "Here HE is!" you think.
Despite the fact that there may be rumors floating about that this guy is a serial dater, or even a serial marrier, suddenly it truly feels as if you are THE ONE for him and vice versa.

As he opens up his injured, little boy side to you, you may become drawn in, and attempt to be the one to heal his wounds.
Why not? He so obviously needs you, and surely he doesn't confide his innermost thoughts, fears, and wounded history to every woman he dates!

He makes it clear to you that no other woman before you has met his standard of beauty, intellect, values, fashion sense, passion, etc. He hints early on at an obvious future together, but also that he needs time to really get to know you so as to avoid the pitfalls of his previous failed relationships.

"Is this real"? Is the question he puts forth time and again, his mouth agape in wonder.

You may become drawn in pretty quickly. You may cast aside your initial doubts, discount the gossip you have heard about him, and throw yourself head first off of the bridge into the shark infested waters of this man's aura.

This narcissistic personality type will of course reveal itself before too much time has gone by. He simply cannot maintain the veneer of supportive, loving potential partner for too long, because first and foremost, his needs take precedence over those of any other creature in the universe.

Just when you feel that it is safe to express some small issue that may have been bothering you.... Let's say that you noticed that he did not text you, or even respond to your text messages, as often as usual, or as quickly as you would have liked or expected... or perhaps he has broken his usual pattern of regularly calling you, or neglected to mention anything about getting together Thursday night, whereas previously, he always did so... and so you decide to mention to him that you have noticed, or been hurt by, any of the above ....WHAMMO!

You get to meet the REAL him.

This guy cannot tolerate any hint of criticism (as he sees it), or doubt about his behaviors and intentions. Therefore he will do the "switcheroo".

He has the unique ability to flip *you* into the role of perpetrator, in any scenario, at anytime, anywhere!
Examples:
You – "what's going on? I didn't hear from you these past couple of days."
Him – "you have been distant and cold all week"!
You –"I feel like maybe you want to date other women."
Him – "Since you are suggesting that we should be dating other people, I don't feel secure in this relationship with you."
Him - " Are you ready to get married?"
You - "I love you and am ready to get engaged."
Him-"Now that you have changed the status quo, I feel under pressure! I thought we were both in a holding pattern."

Essentially, this guy will interpret almost any statement to him as an attack, and he will use this as an excuse to begin the inevitable Withdrawal Phase. This phase is marked by a pulling back on his part, exhibited through lessening the frequency of contact, as well as the loving phrases and actions with which he initially drew you in.

You, previously the one being pursued, fawned over and even obsessed about, are now thrown into the role of pursuer, hopelessly struggling to regain the footing and momentum that you had perceived to be the basis of your relationship.

Suddenly, you may find yourself being the one to text, call, suggest getting together, etc., and him being the one to demurely accept your attentions, picking and choosing when to make himself available.

At this juncture, Mr. Unobtainable is no longer suggesting dates, texting or calling much at all, and you most probably are racking your brains trying to figure out what happened? And more importantly, how do I get back to where we were before?? And then, inevitably, he disappears completely with nary a logical explanation or apology. He is just …. gone.

What was your mistake? What did you do wrong? Can this be fixed?

No girlfriend. This cannot be fixed, because HE cannot be fixed. Only years of therapy, with its resulting self-awareness, could maybe fix him, but since he never realizes that he has a problem, it won't happen, ever!

But really, what did happen? Why did your relationship go from potential-packed excitement to Nada?

Because, as your natural human needs and emotions began to surface, he began to realize that he would be called upon to give to, nurture and accommodate you.

Unfortunately, this man is not capable of those things. Therefore, he had to move on.
Of course, he himself cannot see this reality. In his mind, your needs are "demands", your comments are criticisms, and your desire to be with him is neediness.
Poof! He has moved on!
And so must you.

The Initial Red Flags that this personality type will wave in your face should suffice to warn you well in advance of inevitable heartbreak.
These signs can include:
An unwillingness to plan anything in advance with you - Travel, holidays, weekends away, even a lecture series, can all pose a problem for Mr. Unobtainable, because he truly cannot commit to anything with you if it is more than a day or two in the future.

He will *not* introduce you to friends and family, even if he and you are out together and you happen to bump into his people along the way!

Another major flag factor is the quality of relationships he has with his own family. Look at them closely.
If Mr. Unobtainable reports to you that his wife of 30 years walked out on him with "no warning" and that he has no clue why she would do such a thing since he provided for her and their flock of children so beautifully, please stop right there and ask yourself this:
What woman walks out on a good husband, with no warning or conversation?
A woman, who does walk out with no warning, or conversation, surely felt that she was in either emotional or physical peril. She must have come to the sad realization that there is no complaint she can lodge that he can calmly process and address, no hope for being heard and accommodated.
Only a woman, who has lost all hope, does such an act.

If he mentions to you that his parents, children, uncles, aunts and cousins do not speak to him, and he does not know why, and that they are "all crazy", realize this; he is the crazy one, and not the victim he wants you to perceive him as.

It is only a matter of time before you are his target, as he is ever on the alert for confirmation that he had judged you too favorably.
He needs to feel that he can break it off at any moment, and go on his merry way to the next unsuspecting victim of his charms.

He is not a gift giver.
Here again, his unwillingness to invest in you is a clear sign of a lack of real commitment. Despite the pretty words he lavishes on you, his actions (or inaction) are what tell the real story. However well to do he may be, this charmer prefers not to spend big bucks on you, as a part of him knows all along, you are just one more notch in his belt.

You may ask why?

Why would a good looking and successful man who appears to have it all, be unable to allow his relationship to progress normally towards a rock solid commitment?

The answer lies in his history, and most probably goes back to his childhood.

He may have been hurt/ rejected by his parents in some way, and has learned to over protect himself. His past relationships may have proven painful and so he is too busy licking his wounds to move on toward a happy ending.

Though he may claim to be lonely and longing for his true mate, the reality is that he doesn't trust his own judgment and therefore cannot recognize and trust her.

He continuously scans the relationship for flaws, and of course, eventually will find something, minor though it may be, with which to wrench apart what might have been a great thing.

He just can't help himself. He must and will end it.

Chapter Six

Crazy Psychopath

Mr. Crazy Psycho lurks on the internet scanning the dating sites for prey.

He may choose to pinpoint a vulnerable type such as a single Mom or overweight girl and try to "rock her world".

He creates a persona that appeals to the target and proceeds to engage her attentions until she comes to believe that she has found her "prince".

He works fast, as he must rope her in before his true colors reveal themselves and she runs for the hills.

Case Study:

Attractive, well dressed and seemingly wealthy, he spends the big bucks to win her over quickly, arranging for bouquets of flowers to arrive unexpectedly at her door, even before they have met. He sends limos to pick her up and whisk her off into the city for romantic dinners, where he takes her hands in his, looks into her eyes and pronounces her his soul mate.

From the outset he bombards her with texts, calls, flowers, little trinkets and great dates. It is only a couple of weeks before they are discussing where and when they will marry, as there is no doubt that this was MEANT TO BE.

Her friends are concerned. They have heard that he has been married at least twice before, that he has a drinking problem...they would like her to slow it down a bit...

They ask themselves HOW is this smart savvy professional woman allowing herself to be swept away by a stranger? What do we really know about this guy anyway?

I lived this story with my friend Lauren, and it was ugly.

Lauren was swept up in the excitement and lured by the prospect of being "saved" from her struggle as a single mom. It was easy to push aside her doubts as she and Jay danced cheek to cheek to the music played by the orchestra that he paid to serenade them at the end of a black tie charity event he had hosted in both of their names.

As she mentions her various friends to him, in an effort to familiarize him with her world, he listens carefully, making mental notes, as he intends to isolate her from each and every one of them. Essentially anyone who tries to caution her to take things slowly and get to know more about Mr. Dangerous Psycho will face the risk of getting cut right out of her life.

She seemed to have jumped off the cliff of reason and fallen for all of Jay's ensnaring tactics. At no time did she question his motives, no matter how unnatural the relationship appeared to all of us who loved her and wished her well.

"I love him" was all she would say...

When Lauren met Jay on the internet it took all of 2 weeks before they were talking marriage, and they had not even met yet. He made her believe from the very first text message, that this was fate and that they were destined to be together. No need to waste too much time dating and getting to know each other.

It all seemed too good to be true...

Lauren had come from an affluent home on Long Island. Her late dad had been a professional who provided well for his family. She was a graduate of a top Ivy League school, and featured brains and beauty in abundance. As a hard working single mom with no help at all from, and very little contact with her ex-husband who lived out of state, she tried to do it all, working full time, caring for two young boys, and all the while maintaining some sort of a social life.

Lauren was used to a lot of male attention and never really had to deal with down time as there was usually a guy trying to gain her favor...

But Jay seemed different than the rest! He enjoyed showing off his wealth by lavishing her with gifts, introducing her to some major players in his world and escorting her to galas, and top restaurants as well as to his fabulous home in the Hamptons.

At this point he was very attentive, loving, generous and thoughtful.

She thought she had hit the jackpot.

Lauren soon had Jay spending lots of time at her home with her little boys, and before you knew it, they had taken to calling him "daddy"!

This was beyond odd to all of her friends, but they didn't dare to say a word!

She began bringing Jay with her to the social events she attended. Her friends noticed that there was something a bit off about the guy. At a big party at one of Lauren's friends' homes, one of the guests walked into the kitchen, and found Jay standing in there alone, talking to himself! He was saying "ok dear, let's get the kids and get ready to leave". It was apparent that Jay was rehearsing the lines he needed to say to Lauren because he was uncomfortable and wanted to leave. Was this a tactic he learned in anger management class?

Jay proposed to Lauren with a big beautiful diamond and quickly arranged for an engagement party to which her closest friend was not invited.

Why was her closest friend not invited? Because the friend had tried to caution Lauren to slow it down a bit, and to try to get more background information on the guy. She had reason to believe that he had lied about his age, and wanted Lauren to be sure to look into that. The problem was that when her friend spoke to her on the phone about her concerns, Jay was listening in on the conversation. The next day her friend received an email from Lauren. It accused her of sabotaging and being envious of the relationship, and instructed her to stay away from the engagement party and not to contact Lauren again.

More than hurt and angry about the unwarranted insults to her, the friend was very worried about Lauren's well-being. However, she was not the only one worried. Lauren's mom and sister were worried as well. All who cared about her watched in horror as she plunged into a marriage with a guy about whom the rumors were swirling.

Once they married, things started to reveal themselves pretty quickly. Jay was a paranoid and controlling alcoholic. He would check the navigation system in Lauren's car and demand to know why she had gone to the various destinations recorded there. A typical confrontation would go like this:

Him-"why were you at 123 Maple Rd today?"

She – "uh… that's my dentist's office…"

He also accused her of having an affair with a co-worker she barely knew, and flew into a rage when she denied it in no uncertain terms. He stomped out of the house and drove straight to a bar where he drank himself silly.

Jay would scan the credit card statements and accuse Lauren of making unnecessary expenditures.

Lauren worked harder and harder to prove her love and loyally to Jay but the more she tried, the worse things became. He became verbally and emotionally abusive to both her and her little boys. The final straw was when Jay threatened to destroy both Lauren and her kids. At that point, terrified for their wellbeing, she packed up quickly and ran running to the very friend who had tried so hard to caution her from the outset. Pleading for forgiveness, she asked if she and the boys could seek shelter with the friend. The police were called upon to help hide Lauren's car, as all were certain that Jay posed a real threat and would be stalking them.

It is always a big Red Flag when a man seems *too good to be true*!

Jay showed signs of *paranoid and controlling behaviors* and was clearly in a rush to move the relationship forward so that he could isolate and control Lauren.

Some of Jay's symptoms as defined by Phsyc Central included:

• Suspects, without sufficient basis, that others are exploiting, harming, or deceiving him or her

- Is preoccupied with unjustified doubts about the loyalty or trustworthiness of friends or associates

- Has recurrent suspicions, without justification, regarding fidelity of spouse or sexual partner

This condition is thought to be both biological and environmental, not stemming from any particular set of circumstances. It is difficult to treat, especially since the patient usually does not believe that he has a problem and therefore will not seek out or be open to therapeutic intervention.

The moral here?

Real true love does not happen in an instant, and certainly doesn't happen on the internet, sight unseen.

One should never ignore the feelings of discomfort, or warnings, from the people who really care about you. If they are all picking up on the fact that something is off, then believe it!

Regarding the gossip going around about Jay, if there's smoke, there's fire.

Either do your due diligence, or keep away from "Too Good to be True Crazy Psychopath"

Chapter Seven

The Narcissist

Do you find yourself trying to explain yourself over and over again to your BF?

Perhaps you have been unjustly accused of an unsavory motive or your actions have been criticized by him *yet again*, so you again attempt to carefully go over your deeds, thoughts and actions in an attempt to explain them all and to get him to see the "real you".

You are on the defensive now, trying to prove to him that you are really a well-meaning, well intentioned great girl and not the liar, gold digger, manipulator or cheater that he is insinuating you might be...

Has your boyfriend given you a list of your "offenses" and demanded an apology from you, just when you have called *him* out on a behavior that hurt or confused you?

If you have not done anything to apologize for, and are feeling baffled by this new wrench in the dynamic, don't be!

This "Table turning behavior" is a hallmark of the Narcissist.

The Narcissist cannot bear to see himself fully and clearly and can certainly not bear to perceive any wrong doing on his own part. He cannot accept responsibility for any wrongdoing and he cannot apologize...Therefore he must switch the mode of the conversation, turn the tables and place YOU on the defensive, rather than explain or apologize for his misdeeds.

Did your boyfriend sweep you off your feet with grand gestures, proclaim his love almost from the outset and begin making elaborate plans for your future at breakneck speed?

This is classic narcissistic behavior and is designed to rein you in before you have a chance to experience his true nature and his darker side.
The side which needs to maintain control over you and everything else in his environment.

The poor fellow cannot feel safe unless he is in total control and it takes every bit of effort, in the earliest stage of your relationship, for him to feign flexibility and largess.
This stage does not last long and it belongs to the *"Get the Girl "*phase of the relationship.

In that blissful, initial "Get the Girl "phase of your relationship, when he is working hard to procure you, he will flatter you incessantly. He will wine and dine you. He will shower you with love and attention and make plans for you two to be together, permanently, ASAP.

Ahhh.. if only this dreamy phase would go on forever...

For it is quickly followed by the *"devalue the girl"* phase, once he has won your heart and you have become vulnerable to him.
That is when the criticisms and accusations against you will begin.

If he can weaken your ego and make you feel worthless, then he can more easily control you, doling out the praise and goodies when you "deserve" them, and withholding them when you don't.

You will try to defend and explain yourself to him but your words will fall on deaf ears for he cannot internalize or empathize with the thoughts and feelings of another. You will find yourself scurrying around trying to win back his favor, even though you have no clue why you lost it!

If you have met a Narcissist, then just when you are convinced that your prince has finally come along and you two are about to ride off into the sunset, he will burst that bubble.

Quite simply, once he has you he can no longer keep up the charade of MR. NICE GUY.

His veneer will crack *and so will your heart*, if you aren't careful.

When encountering a prince on a white horse swooping you up in his loving arms, please stop and evaluate the situation realistically.

This behavior is classic Narcissistic behavior and if you fall for it, you will suffer greatly.

The male Narcissist only has eyes for one glorious, fabulous person, and that is himself!

He is not looking to please anyone but himself, and he is totally cool with doing whatever he has to do to have his needs met no matter how it may affect another person. In fact, should his girlfriend express a need or desire which conflicts with his own, he may fly into a rage and even go so far as to accuse her of being ungrateful, a complainer or having a personality disorder! That is how threatening it is for him to have his "authority" or wisdom challenged.

He is like an emotional sieve that can never be filled, though mountains of love and attention may be poured into him. His void remains.

The object of his desire will be one who he believes "fills him up" because she enhances his vision of himself, through her beauty, brains, accomplishments or notoriety. He looks better because he has her on his arm.

This Red Flag Man will commence the pursuit by galloping into her life like her knight in shining armor. He will flatter her, objectify her, wine and dine her and promise her the world. He will profess undying love and adoration and will sweep her off her feet until she is giddy with happiness and completely under his spell. Once he has succeeded in capturing her heart, his desire will begin to wane. His attentions, calls and dates will taper off. He may shun her for days, take umbrage at the slightest remark, explode in anger unexplainably and then slink off into his cave with nary a care as to how this all may affect her.

Once he has secured her love and affection, he will inevitably get bored and lonely again, and then discard his once treasured partner.

Your emotional pain means nothing to this man. He can't begin to relate to it. Moreover, he takes no responsibility for anything that goes wrong between you and will go over your interactions with a fine tooth comb in an effort to find fault with everything you have said or done. You alone are to blame for the waning of his interest and desire in you as he is always the perfect, innocent victim.

This personality blossomed within him as a result of damage to his sense of security as a child. Either a rejecting or abandoning parent taught this man not to trust or, parents who exaggerated his greatness and left him with the delusion that he deserves the best of everything, whilst his subconscious mind knew better. Thus he seeks to tamp down the ever present doubt within him that he is Mr. Wonderful.

It is our parents who teach us that we are valuable and lovable by displaying their consistent love and concern. Their reliable nurturing and protection teaches us that we are worthy of love. If they fail in this task by withholding that love and attention, or offering us empty praise not accompanied by true attention and affection, then we learn that we are unworthy of love and that we cannot depend on people. We have not acquired the basic ability to trust, since our primary caretakers were not there for us emotionally or physically.

A narcissist will seek out a partner to love and to fill the aching void within him, but never really trust the love he finds, nor respect it.

The narcissist opts to exercise a great deal of self-care as a way of preserving his psychological well-being. He must parent himself, at anyone's expense. He is the center of his universe and is neither capable of nor interested in empathizing with another.

Several of the Red Flag men presented here have an aspect of narcissism. These include the Unobtainable Dream Boat, Married Man Seeking Upgrade, and Crazy Psychopath.

Life with the narcissist means that you will be placating him, satisfying him, and obeying him, often at the expense of your own dreams and desires. He regards your differing viewpoints and wishes as betrayals, because in his eyes you are nothing more than an extension of him. You cannot disagree with him, nor have your own individual desires, any more than a solider can unilaterally opt to do his own thing in defiance of his captain.

A relationship with a narcissist will be a roller coaster ride. His Jekyll and Hyde personality switches in a flash, and throws one off balance. The intermittent highs will be mitigated by the terrible lows and will inflict untold suffering to the spirit.
When he finally dashes your heart to bits, he will gallop off again, leaving you alone to pick up the pieces.

TELLTALE SIGNS OF NARCISSITIC PERSONALITY DISORDER (From the Diagnostic and Statistical Manual of Mental Disorders, Fifth Edition, 2013)

Narcissism is indicated by a pattern of behaviors and needs.
(If your guy has five or more of the following traits then he is a Red Flag Man):

Has an inflated sense of self-importance (e.g., exaggerates achievements and talents, expects to be recognized as superior without commensurate achievements).
Is preoccupied with fantasies of unlimited success, power, brilliance, beauty, or ideal love.
Believes that he is "special" and unique and can only be understood by, or should associate with, other special or high-status people (or institutions).
Requires excessive admiration.
Has a sense of entitlement (i.e., unreasonable expectations of especially favorable treatment or automatic compliance with his or her expectations).
Is interpersonally exploitative (i.e., takes advantage of others to achieve his or her own ends).
Lacks empathy: is unwilling to recognize or identify with the feelings and needs of others.
Is often envious of others or believes that others are envious of him or her.
Shows arrogant, haughty behaviors or attitudes.

Chapter Eight

The Red Flag Man – Big Age Difference

Marlene had grown into a stunning young woman and was about to enter college. She was looking forward to having a bit of freedom from her parents, and enjoying the dating scene unfettered by their strict, rather old fashioned household rules.

Marlene's parents had a bachelor friend who liked to come and visit from time to time. One of those guys who had devoted his life to his work, become very successful, and had now reached his late 40's without having married or had a family. Spending time with Marlene's family gave him a sense of belonging as he lived alone and was starting to feel the emptiness.

Josh had gotten into a routine of spending most Sundays with Marlene's family, joining them for picnics, BBQs and other family outings. He came around and stayed around so much that gossip began to swirl around that Josh had a "thing" for Marlene's attractive Mother.
The reality was, he had developed a "thing" for 18 year old Marlene!

While she had thought she was just indulging him, and being polite when she accompanied him bike riding or playing tennis, he was busy falling head over heels in love with her.

Soon enough a situation had developed. Josh realized that this was the woman he wanted to make his life with.

Now he had to approach her parents with the shocking news that he had fallen in love with their daughter, who was 27 years younger than him.

"But what about the age difference?" They responded. "What kind of a life will our daughter have with a man old enough to be her father?"

Josh replied that if he could have even 10 good years with Marlene, his life would be worth living.
He planned on devoting himself to her and her happiness.

Marlene was caught up in the excitement of being adored by a wealthy and accomplished older man. Next the two of them began pressuring her parents for their blessing to marry.

Josh presented Marlene with a huge diamond ring.
Flowers and presents began arriving at the home.
The parents consented despite their reservations, and a fabulous wedding was planned for all of their friends and family.

Once all of the celebrations were over, the new couple settled into life together in their luxury NYC apartment. Marlene kept busy decorating and shopping, until she became pregnant with their first child, and then their second.
Summers were spent in the Hamptons
Winter vacations were spent skiing in the French Alps.
Life was good.

As the years passed, friends noticed that Marlene's facial expression had started to become a bit strained...
At social gatherings she sometimes seemed to disparage and disrespect her husband. She let comments slip about the infrequency of their sex life. It seemed that the age difference had begun to take its toll on her.

Apparently, the wealth and luxury that she enjoyed as the wife of an older, successful business man did not compensate for the shortcomings in their union. She was frustrated with her husband as he began to slow down, travel less, and have less need for intimacy with her. His views on things diverged from her own in many areas, including the raising of their children, and resentment began to build up.

The couple stayed together, but the situation had left her bitter and angry. Joshua eventually fell ill, and passed away, leaving Marlene a widow with two teenage boys, at the age of 33.

Chapter Nine

The Passive Pot Head

Such a handsome, nice guy!
Wow! How lucky Bonnie was to have this guy living right up the block!
After bumping into each other a few times in the neighborhood, they very naturally fell into a pattern of going for long walks, and eventually graduated to hanging out together to watch TV.

Though they started out as neighbors, there was clearly potential there for a relationship, or so she thought….

Mr. Nice Neighbor was pretty good company.
He was reliable, had his own little business, owned his own nice house, and enjoyed helping Bonnie out with tasks around her home.
Soon enough they were officially dating, which meant that Bonnie was the gal he asked to join him, whenever he was invited over to his friend's house for a party.

She didn't really mind much that he preferred to get high before each outing, and oh yeah, after each outing as well. It didn't seem to affect his intellect, which she admired, or his ability to function. In her mind he was sexy, smelled good and was good for a mediocre roll in the hay.
Little by little the two of them developed feelings for each other.

After a few years of this, Mr. Nice Neighbor suggested that Bonnie movie into his home.
He felt that he was a better man with her on board, and he'd have liked to keep her around.
The problem was, his place was in a kind of a time warp! He hadn't cleaned up for years, and the furnishings and paint job all dated back to the time when his home had been his parent's place, the home he grew up in and took over after his folks died.

His yard was littered with the remains of odd jobs he had tinkered with over the years; several lawn mowers from his stint as a landscaping guy, a couple of rusting motorcycles and an old car or two. His dogs and cats and pet rabbit all seemed comfortable enough, but Bonnie is a classy gal and found the place kind of Yuk!

So she started to suggest to him that she would love to spend some more time there, if only he would clean the place up.

He accommodated her by painting at least one floor of the home, but was not inclined to do more than that.
Since his teen years he had inhabited the basement of the home, and despite his invite to Bonnie to move in with him, he seemed oddly reticent to move upstairs, either figuratively or literally.
Meaning, he was reluctant to clean up his act, and progress to a higher/ adult level of life style.
The years slipped by.
Bonnie broke it off with him from time to time as she tired of hearing her family and friends suggest that she could do better, and she became frustrated by his reluctance to tune into her needs and feelings.
The truth is, she loved him, but not passionately, and she didn't suffer all that much when apart from him. Complacency had come to define their relationship altogether.

They would break up and then make up again whenever he got sexually "pent up" enough to come knocking on her door with promises that things would get better. He loved Bonnie and wanted to make it work.
The two of them spent time together and shared holidays with family and friends. She was happy to go out together, and they made a fine looking couple, since he had finally allowed her to clean up his act somewhat, and he cleaned up real nice!

No he was not her intellectual or spiritual match, but he was nice to have around! If she could only get him to function on a somewhat higher level, he might make a nice husband... However, she never really pictured herself living with a pot- smoking high school dropout, kicking aside plumbing parts as he rambled around his parent's old home.

"Let's decorate this place" she would suggest.

THE RED FLAG MAN

But he wasn't much motivated and kind of tuned her out. The most he would offer to do is to apply a fresh coat of paint.

"Let's move you up out of this basement. She pleaded. You have a whole big beautiful house we could fix up and live in together"- but he said that things were cool the way they were.

The truth is that the years of heavy pot smoking had left him without a shred of motivation to improve or change anything at all in his life.
Yeah he'd enjoy having Bonnie around more, but if her terms included the need for him to evolve at all, well that wasn't happening!

His inertia came to define the relationship as he proved unable to plan for or prepare a future with her. He was only capable of living in the present, and would have liked Bonnie along for the ride.

Bonnie ached as she realized the lost potential there, but she knew she had to face reality. She had been wasting years of her life going back and forth with a guy who was stuck in his teen years. An overgrown hippie for whom everything was:

"Copacetic" "Peace" "Love"

It was time for Bonnie to move on!
Mr. Nice Neighbor was going nowhere fast.
Unless she wanted to spend the rest of her days with a bong-head whose idea of a perfect date was sharing a bowl of chips with her on the couch watching old movies, she had to skedaddle!

Nice just isn't enough girls!

How had he wound up stuck like this as the rest of his class moved on with their lives?
He was probably raised by liberal, hard working parents that taught him that it is commendable to "do your own thing", or perhaps he rebelled against overly strict conservative parents. Whatever it was, he was in the habit of self medicating with Pot to take the edge off.
He had tried to grow up and do the head of the household/ responsible parent thing, but had had some disappointments with his life, marriage, and relationships and wound up happier just learning to inhale.

He learned not to take life too seriously and not to dig deeply into his emotions or those of others. Better to skim over the surface of life like a stone on a pond.

Eventually he stayed stoned for good.

In his stoned state, he was incapable of, and uninterested in emotionally connecting with another. As such, he could not offer true love or much more than a commitment of convenience.

What were the tattered Red Flags blowing in this guy's breeze?

Lots of Pot smoking

Inertia

(He had zero desire to move forward in his life or in his relationship)

Lack of motivation to do anything to please or satisfy a desire of another

(His tude was take me as is or leave me.)

Bye Bye to this guy!

Chapter Ten

The Too Much Too Soon Looney Tune

Dashingly handsome, polished and dressed to the nines, Mr. TMTS asked Rachel if she would join him for a coffee date or a walk in the park, when they met at a social event for which she had flown into NYC to attend.

Off the bat she noticed that he seemed just a bit awkward socially, and even a tad sad...his speech being slow and deliberate, his smile a bit forced. Something about him aroused her empathy...and even though she would soon be headed back home to Florida, her interest was piqued enough to give this a go.

He was a musician/composer/conductor of impeccable credentials, for whom work was becoming ever more elusive. As such he had plenty of spare time on his hands to woo and win Rachel, then claim her as his own, all within 24 hours!

Their first date/serenade, was titillating as he "sees "in music and described Rachel as a Mozart concerto. He was "taken " by her charm, yet revealed that he was still a bit broken over the rough ending of his last courtship, just weeks before. His former GF ran a knife through his soul and carved out his flesh with her cruelty, but that did not stop him from shooting Rachel a quick email the morning after their first date, informing her that he now "loved HER for all eternity".

He gallantly escorted Rachel around town, hailing cabs like a pro and whispering seductively in her ear as they whizzed off to a candlelit dinner downtown. It was truly romantic, and sad for her to face the prospect of parting from this dude. But Logistics don't daunt him! He would court her from afar, promising to visit soon, while bemoaning the expense involved.

Shouldn't all this have sufficed to warn Rachel of his impetuous/artistic nature?

Nope!

She chose to give him the benefit of the doubt, and here is what she went on to experience over the ensuing days and weeks:

A flurry of texts, calls and emails vowing undying love, and eternal commitment, (minus any practical suggestion as to where and how the two of them would live, or on what?), an urgent need to connect with her at all hours of the day and night, pre-dawn requests to hear her voice, overtly explicit Face Time sessions (proudly displaying his junk), depressive rantings amidst tears for the late/great heroes of our time, (He was prone to wailing in sorrow wondering why the life of JFK had been cut short whereas his own worthless ass was still alive),euphoria followed by despair, hints of suicidal tendencies, a sprinkling of cruelty, lewd crude text messages, TMI about the anatomy of the last GFs nether parts (ewww), poetry, flowers, postcards, and promises, in old English or French. (At times he seemed to have been dropped into the wrong century entirely. A relic from the Renaissance.)

The denouement?

A proposal of marriage, just 5 dates into their relationship!

He inflated his bank account and professional prospects, and then cried about his fears of being penniless and alone.

In a matter of a few days he had projected his fantasy of the perfect love onto Rachel, though he could not yet have really gotten to know her! He even created his own tender nicknames for her, thus creating an artificial intimacy not borne of time and experience, but rather of a sense of urgency, emptiness and need.

Despite the deep connection and undying love he professed for Rachel, he soon became quick to lash out at her for any minor perceived infraction.

An innocent "how do you see us working logistically?" was met with an angry "Don't nag me! I told you I would do whatever I had to do to make this work!"

Somehow the weeks slipped by with nary a mention of him visiting her in Florida...

He lamented his chosen career path, as it had not provided him much of a financial cushion. He had never owned a home, but had traveled the world as a nomad, going from one musical stint to the next, country to country, city to city, performing his concerts, and then returning to a lonely pension hotel.

His relationships had faltered as well, and it eventually became obvious that he lacked the emotional tool set to maintain them. Though his artistic contribution had been great, on a personal level, he had nothing to show for it at all. A truth that left him in the grip of despair, in between bouts of euphoria over his new found love.

As he revealed more and more about himself to Rachel, she learned that his last GF was a wealthy Cougar, who had been more than happy to install him into her 5th Avenue digs, sponsor a concert or two for him, connect him to her powerful friends in high society and outfit him from head to toe. He lamented the loss of his foothold into the older, richer lady's good graces.

Still his tenderness compelled Rachel forward anyway, in the hopes of a fairy tale ending which would never come.

It can take time to ascertain whether one is dealing with mental illness, an artistic drama queen, a "Dandy" or a once in a life time love story; that is of course unless one has read The Red Flag Man!

Had Rachel read this book, she would have recognized The Dependent Personality! The Gigolo! She would have recognized the possibility of Bi Polar Disorder!
She would have stayed away!

From Wikipedia,
"A gigolo is a male escort or social companion who is supported by a woman in a continuing relationship, often living in her residence or having to be present at her beck and call. The gigolo is expected to provide companionship, to serve as a consistent escort with good manners and social skills, and often, to serve as a dancing partner as required by the woman in exchange for the support (which is contrary to typical norms). Many gifts such as expensive clothing and an automobile to drive may be lavished upon him. The relationship may include sexual services as well, when he also would be referred to as "a kept man".
The term gigolo usually implies a man who adopts a lifestyle consisting of a number of such relationships serially, rather than having other means of support.

Mr. TMTS Looney Toon may actually be quite attracted to you, even earnestly interested in you. However, unless you are in a position to support him in the long run, he will most likely remain on the prowl. He will keep his options open, as he trawls for his next meal ticket and is not above surreptitiously contacting an ex GF whilst wooing you, if he perceives a chance in hell of getting back onto her gravy train.

In fact Rachel discovered that her earnest musical lover had been in regular contact with his "ex" the entire time they were together! He was playing both horses in his race towards the hoped for big win.

If you pull away before he is ready to let you go, you can expect desperate and even threatening attempts to cling to the emotional life line you have become to him.

So, how to recognize Mr. TMTS Looney Toon?
The sad reality is that "Too Good to be true" is just that. Instant eternal love is an unlikely scenario. Wild mood swings ranging from euphoria to despair, and marriage proposals coming after an insanely short time dating are most likely a sign of personality disorder, and/ or a desperate need to attach to another, for any number of reasons.
Reality Check!
It's NOT REAL

Chapter Eleven

Long Distance Scammer/Charmer

It took a detective's report to finally motivate Joy to dump the lying scammer she had picked up on the internet and was now almost engaged to.

He had wooed her from afar, flying coast to coast to sweep her off her feet. His tactics included portraying himself as a partner in a successful medical technology company, the single father of two well- adjusted boys, and an all-around nice guy bent on winning her heart with trips, romance and a Cartier watch.

She, a single mom, lonely and bored on Long Island, had trolled the internet dating sites one evening and got caught up in a conversation with this pleasant looking dude in California; he too, a single parent looking for love after a messy divorce.

They clicked, and went on to keep up a casual convo by phone and email over the next weeks, until he told her that he was coming to NY on business, and wanted to get together.

He was pretty cute in person and seemed to have lots more in common with Joy than she had realized. He made sure that he appeared to be exactly what she had been looking for.

Vulnerable to the prospect of a new loving relationship after a heart breaking break up, she took him at face value, believing whatever he told her.

They met just as she was about to purchase a house in the suburbs. Not surprisingly, he told her that he could conduct his business from anywhere, as it was computer based, so moving his family to NY would be no problem at all. They could all live happily together!

He pursued her from near and far, buying her gifts and ingratiating himself into her life.

She made a trip to LA to meet his family and discovered that he actually lived in his mom's house with his 2 boys. It was the home he had grown up in, and the natural place for him to return to after his divorce. The place was a terrible mess. The home had gone to pot, the property unkempt.

Joy noticed that his boys lied easily. His ex-wife came around in a fit of temper. Lots of his stories didn't add up. As time went on she caught him in a couple of pretty big whoppers.

Yet, despite the numerous negative and even fishy aspects Joy had discovered, for some reason she was not inclined to break it off with the California charmer.

It wasn't until her parents shared their own doubts with a private detective friend of theirs that the ugly facts would have to be confronted.

Posing as "Carol", a wealthy business owner, the 65 year old male detective succeeded in luring Mr. Scammer Charmer into what he would think was the beginning of a promising new relationship with a wealthy woman. A convenient back up in case Joy failed to take the bait.

Meanwhile, the detective also pulled a credit check as well as a background report, revealing that Mr. Charmer's history was a financial nightmare featuring numerous foreclosures, multiple addresses and failed business ventures.

Worst of all, "Charmer man" was making plans with "Carol" while romancing Joy in NY, and feeling like he had hit "pay dirt!"
Little did he know that "Carole" was a male detective sitting on his computer in NJ and bent on exposing him for the lying cheater he really was.

When presented with the sordid facts, Joy quickly broke off the relationship, only to find herself inundated with emails and calls demanding that she return the fancy watch and other presents charmer boy had given her. His emails had a bit of a threatening tone which creeped her out all the more. She returned the watch to him, blocked his calls and emails and thanked her parents for their due diligence.

This is another true story illustrating the perils of long distance love. Romancing from afar leaves too many unknowns.

Chapter Twelve

The Powerless Puppet

He was charming, good looking, rich, intelligent and single.

He was following Linda around like an enamored puppy.

He was loyal, and wanted nothing more than to please Linda in every way.

It would have been great, if only she could have snipped the umbilical cord still dangling from his belly and connected to his miserable, miserly, mean mom!

Sometimes we meet up with a man who technically and for all practical purposes is available, and who In fact is very much interested in marrying and starting a family. However, he answers to a Higher Authority - his mom and dad.

The Powerless Puppet is not in a position to call the shots in his own life, because Mom and Pops control the purse strings. Even worse, they don't respect their son, and are convinced that any woman, who may appear to be interested in him, must be a gold digger with an evil agenda. Thus they will rally against her at every turn, undermining the stability of their son's relationship with their insinuations and suspicions.

Years of living like this can wear down any couple.

It is exceedingly hard to make a life with a man who has never cut the ties with his parents and who never became financially independent. His male ego has suffered a blow from which it will never fully recover. Though one may wish to believe that she and he can go off into the sunset and create their own new independent family unit, this man has never developed the skills to carve out his own destiny. He has been emasculated since birth, and can only function as a dependent and needy creature masquerading as a regular guy.

The tragedy is that a woman, who does indeed start out loving and respecting such a man, eventually will come to resent his inability to function independently, and ultimately she will want to abandon him, thus proving his parents suspicions correct! Their son cannot head up his own household. Their son does not merit a loving devoted wife.

My friend Linda lived this story, and she asked me to include it as a precautionary tale.

Linda and Jon met at a social event in their local community center. Linda had recently moved to this country from South Africa, was working as a school teacher, and was on the hunt for a nice husband.
She had come from a prominent family and was looking for a partner of a similar background.

Jon was a fine young man from a wealthy NY family. He moved in the highest echelons of society and was on the lookout for his life's partner. Attracted to Linda's natural grace, beauty and refined manners, he asked her out for dinner.

Jon revealed to Linda that he had suffered a brain injury as a child, and that he now had to live on anti-seizure meds. As such, he was not licensed to drive a car. Luckily his parents had arranged a position for him in the family business and so he was able to live comfortably and function independently from them…. Or so Linda believed…

Just days before their wedding, unbeknownst to Linda, Jon's parents insisted that he accompany them to the family lawyer's office, where he was made to sign his assets over to his mother, in order to "protect him".

From the get- go this couple faced a financial as well as physical handicap, as Jon's hands were now tied financially. He could incur no major expense without the approval of his parents, who questioned and criticized almost every expenditure.

Instead of appreciating their daughter in law, Jon's parents proved to be a constant source of strain on the couple, with their unrelenting criticisms, financial withholding and emotionally detached demeanor.

When Jon faced a health crisis, his parents failed to be supportive, insisting that Linda deal with it herself, since she had "chosen him".

The years went by, two children were born, and Jon lost his position in the family business when it was sold. The young family was now entirely dependent on the in-laws for everything they needed.

Unable to maintain the quality of life she had been accustomed to, without a partner she could rely on for help and support with the daily chores, children, and responsibilities, as well as the frequent health issues, and absent parents, Linda began to fall apart. She no longer saw Jon as a husband/partner.
In her eyes he had become like another dependent child.

At last the moment arrived when she could take it no more and she announced that she had had enough and wanted out.
Jon's parents quickly arranged to pick up him along with his possessions; smugly reminding him that it was for this very situation that they had "protected" his assets so many years ago.

Jon was installed back into his childhood room in his parents' home.

Without his wife and children he quickly grew depressed, and then physically ill. Within 2 years he was dead.

The warning signs?
The powerless puppet seeks the approval and financial back up of others, and he always will. Do not be swept off your feet by the illusion of a lifestyle that he cannot independently provide. Do not believe that he will develop the strength to be his own man. If his parents installed a dependency chip in him at birth, then he ultimately will return to them like a homing pigeon, even at the cost of his inevitable self-destruction. If he is a man who cannot function unless bolstered and supported by others, then this is a disaster course for a woman looking for a normal, healthy, functioning partner.

Chapter Thirteen

Beware the User/Loser!

The User/Loser has a simple agenda: Locate and Latch Onto a woman who can take care of him financially.

He will enter the relationship posing as far more accomplished and successful than he actually is, in an effort to wow and win her.

He buys expensive gifts, arranges trips, and takes her to the best restaurants. This is the *staging phase* of the relationship in which he must set up a false scenario of his financial security and cool factor.

He most probably will appear to be tuned in to and attentive to her every need. He flatters her, has a way of making her feel young, beautiful, unique and desired. But here's the kicker... Once sucked in by this guy the whole dynamic changes overnight as the User /Loser is not prepared to provide anything at all, long term.
He actually is a needy and non- functional parasite who hopes to latch onto and ultimately suck the life out of his host.

This type has never succeeded in his field or perhaps has never even nailed down a specific field of work. He does not own property or assets, and may even be heavily in debt.
In a Pinch he will take back the gifts he has given you so that he can pay off a debt.

Once entrapped by Mr. Loser/User, it is all over for you. He will rely on/use you for everything.
You will provide the stability, financial resources, common sense, social connections, etc.

Whatever he needs will come right out of your hide, so hide if you can from User Loser Man!

How to identify him?
He is not gainfully employed and has ample time to concentrate on you and you alone.
He does not own anything of substance and may even live with his mother or some other relative.
He will talk with you late into the night, sharing his hopes and dreams for a future with the heretofore undiscovered girl of his dreams.
He is a chameleon who will willingly morph into whatever you need him to be, just to get you to the altar.
Once there, Game Over.

His true colors come out and he reveals himself to be the disappointing under-achiever you were taught to avoid.

He is capable of borrowing money from everyone in your social circle, draining your savings and mortgaging the home to fund the lifestyle you both crave but to which he cannot contribute. He is delusional and incapable of confronting the simple realty that one has to work to earn and enjoy the good life.

Be careful because your credit, assets, reputation and sanity are all at stake here.

This man's agenda is specifically tailored to getting his needs met, no matter what the cost to you. Your financial, emotional and physical wellbeing are not taken into consideration as he plows ahead with his oft times detrimental agenda.

He will think nothing of asking for help with even the most mundane of tasks, rather than just taking care of matters himself.

His attitude is "the world owes me".

It can take months or even years for the full impact of this man's alliance with you to be fully revealed, so it is of the utmost importance that you are keenly aware of the Red Flags here right from the outset.

How to spot him?

Hey, the Red Flags are always there!

These may include:
Inconsistent work patterns- he has too much free time.
He is a middle age man who owns nothing, or a young man who should be farther along on his career path , and should be living independent of his parents, but isn't.
When presented with opportunities requiring some serious hard work on his part, he tends to shy away, issuing some lame excuse or downplaying the potential that is obviously right there before your eyes.
He may involve you in helping him to take advantage of an opportunity by requesting your help in every aspect of whatever work or preparation is involved.
He seems to need help and advice before making any decision, and often has a "committee" of his peers with whom he feels compelled to consult.

A conversation with this man may feel more like a ping pong game than an intelligent discourse, if it involves you making a suggestion to him on how to further his career.

Here is a little vignette to illustrate what I mean:
You – "I'm thinking that you should explore the idea of going into the ---- business since you have a lot of knowledge about –-"
Him – "can you write up a business proposal for me??"
You – "but I have never written a business proposal before!"
Him – "That's ok, write something up and I will doc it up"

So you write something up and then:
Him: "can you please call those friends of yours who have been in the ---- biz before and ask them for their contacts?"
You: "No, I am not comfortable doing that. You call them"
Him: "Can I have their email and their numbers please? Can you ask them if it's ok for me to call? Can I invite them here and you'll prepare dinner for them...etc?"

In short – *whatever IT is*, will require your constant support, input, oversight, contacts, efforts, financial help, etc.
He simply will never be inclined to independently take an idea and just run with it.
You may very well find yourself eventually receiving embarrassing negative feedback from any friends or contacts that you have connected him with,

because he will incessantly badger them for their feedback and support as well.

How did he become like this?
Perhaps he came from a family who had low expectations of him, or were themselves underachievers. Maybe his dad relied on his mom to support the family while he pursued pipe dreams or dozed on the sofa.
Maybe his parents allowed him to be overly dependent on them. As a result he never had to learn the art of independent survival. However, he has on occasion tasted the good life and now needs to find someone who can fill the shoes of the mommy and daddy who used to provide it for him.

He is a "Dependent Personality" type.
Look out for the following, as defined by Psych Central:
"• Has difficulty making everyday decisions without an excessive amount of advice and reassurance from others
• Needs others to assume responsibility for most major areas of his or her life
• Has difficulty expressing disagreement with others because of fear of loss of support or approval
• Has difficulty initiating projects or doing things on his or her own (because of a lack of self-confidence in judgment or abilities rather than a lack of motivation or energy)
• Goes to excessive lengths to obtain nurturance and support from others, to the point of volunteering to do things that are unpleasant

• Feels uncomfortable or helpless when alone because of exaggerated fears of being unable to care for himself or herself
• Urgently seeks another relationship as a source of care and support when a close relationship ends
• Is unrealistically preoccupied with fears of being left to take care of himself
Exhibits an inappropriate and chronic reliance on another individual for their health, subsistence, decision making or personal and emotional well-being
If a parent, may exhibit Parentification - A form of role reversal, in which a child is inappropriately given the role of meeting the emotional or physical needs of the parent or of the family's other children.
Self-Victimization - Casting oneself in the role of a victim.
Sense of Entitlement - An unrealistic, unmerited or inappropriate expectation of favorable living conditions and favorable treatment at the hands of others.

Stalking - Any pervasive and unwelcome pattern of pursuing contact with another individual.
Testing - Repeatedly forcing another individual to demonstrate or prove their love or commitment to a relationship.

It is very appropriate for children to follow their parents and to be dependent on them for guidance and support. Once they become mature adults, they must learn to be independent and self-supporting. However, in Dependent Personality Disorder, the individual fails to master independence; he hence remains dependent on others for guidance and support.

Yikes!
Run his credit if you can and then run away from User/Loser Man!

Chapter Fourteen

Red Flag Man – The Misogynist

This man's game is often very hard to spot at the beginning. It involves seeking out a female partner to win over and ultimately dominate, in a relationship in which he retains full control.
In this manner he is able to feel safe and secure.

He comes from a heart wrenching past in which his mother abused, abandoned or rejected him. His childhood was fraught with anguish and despair as he could not depend on the very figure that a child naturally relies on for nurturing and love.
Since as a child he had never experienced life as a valued, unconditionally loved person, he seeks a girlfriend/wife to fill his emotional void, but is conflicted between his desire to connect, and his fear of, and anger at women.

The rage towards his mother is always simmering just beneath the surface of his conscious mind. He cannot and will not trust any woman. After all, if his own mother could hurt and abandon him, how can he trust any other woman not to do the same? He fears that if he loves a woman, she may take him over. If he loves a woman, he may become dependent upon her. This is too scary for the man whose experience with female love is that of being hurt and abandoned by she who should have loved him first and best.

This man may smirk at the notion that you might know more than him about any topic at all, even if the topic is one you have been schooled in and he has not.
He must be the boss/master at all times, and is enraged by a woman's suggestion that she may possess insights or information that he does not.

This Red Flag man is not easy to recognize until significant time has passed, and of course, your heart may already be roped into him by the time you realize what he is all about.

He will court you like a true gentleman and charm the socks off of you in the initial romancing phase. But eventually he must establish total control, and that is when the problems will begin.

Little criticisms will begin to occur with more and more frequency and are intended to weaken the woman's ego and create self-doubt, so that she will be more inclined to surrender control to her "stronger, more capable" partner.

He uses manipulation to control the dynamics of the relationship and has no problem lying to you, cheating on you, and switching moods at the snap of a finger. (All of which, by the way, are your fault!)

His rage is set off if he perceives criticism, any hint of rejection, (even where there is none intended) or if his ideas are challenged in any way.

He must maintain control at all costs because loss of control is too dangerous for him. His circumstances must be controlled by him at all times so as to avoid being hurt again.

He is a tormented soul who dreads loneliness and isolation yet keeps creating distance from others.
He does not want to be questioned, second guessed, or contradicted. He will explode in anger and lash out in rage if he feels that he is being given less than total respect and obedience.

It is his way or the highway.

In his anger he may blurt out a horrible insult that he will later deny saying. Not only will he deny it, he will accuse you of having a faulty memory with no basis in reality. You are "hearing things".

He might line up another woman to have waiting in the wings lest he feels a hint of rejection from you. He is capable of walking out, rather than talking out, any issue on the table.

While you are waiting and pining away for the man who just yesterday promised you the moon and the stars, he has moved on to his next conquest with no explanation. If pressed he may tell you that you pushed him away.

He is a sad figure indeed, because although his happiest times are when the two of you are together, laughing and loving, he cannot sustain those times for more than a few days. He feels engulfed, and must create drama, stress and separation in order to retreat from and then re -enter the relationship, unconsciously recreating the childhood drama/pattern of acceptance followed by rejection that he suffered through as a young boy.

When Betsy met Carl she was swept off her feet pretty quickly. His cute demeanor and boyish charm delighted and excited her.

He was impulsive and generous. Carl thought nothing of getting on a plane and surprising Betsy in NYC only a week after they met in Miami!
It took a month of really fabulous dating until the first signs of the Misogynist began to surface.

It all started with a cup of tea...
Betsy had prepared a lavish dinner for Carl and his son in her home, and was very excited to host them for the very first time, at a point when their budding relationship was a great source of joy to her. She was elated and very much in love.

At the end of the meal Carl wandered into the kitchen and was watching Betsy prepare the tea.
"That's not the correct way to prepare tea" he remarked.

Betsy was not happy to be criticized and felt policed by Carl but she waited until they were seated outside relaxing on her terrace, before deciding to say something about it.
Then she expressed to Carl that she was a grown women with years of experience preparing and serving meals for friends and family and that she didn't like feeling like she had a supervisor hovering about doing "quality control". She told Carl that if he needed to control every aspect of the preparations, or to try to mold her into his ideal of a woman, that he may be happier with an 18 year old girl who had no life experience and could be molded by him into whatever he wanted.

Carl listened quietly and then stepped off the terrace and into the living room. Betsy assumed they would both cool off a bit and resume the conversation and sort things out. However, after 5 minutes Betsy's son stepped out onto the terrace and informed Betsy that Carl and his son had left!

No goodbye, no thank you for dinner – they were gone!

Betsy contacted Carl and suggested that they talk. The very next night he came over, and they talked it out while their boys had pizza in front of the TV.

It seemed that Carl had felt dismissed and rejected by Betsy so he just took off. He told her that he would never leave her again, but she had to promise to never ever suggest that he go to another woman (such as the 18 year old girl she had commented might better suit him).
Betsy assured Carl that she loved him and she would be way more careful of how she spoke to him in the future, and so they seemed to be on track again.

Betsy tried to work with Carl's nature because she really loved him. She enjoyed his warm and charming side and tried to hold onto that, but she soon found that she was unable to predict when something would set him off. He would stomp out of her home without warning, not call for days, would hang up on her in mid conversation, and would then refuse to discuss the issues at hand.

Only when she agreed to get back together with no discussion of their issues, were they able to move on for a short while, before the next eruption.

Carl often made Betsy feel that she was doing or saying the wrong thing. She genuinely tried to avoid those "wrong things" in an effort to keep them on an even keel as a couple, but somehow, the list of "wrong things" kept growing, and despite her trying to avoid any subject that might upset him, it never worked for long.
Betsy eventually began to get a sense that Carl may be playing out his childhood dramas, but realized that he himself had no self-awareness at all. He much preferred to try to convince her that it was she who had issues, who was imagining things, and who needed therapy.

The more she was exposed to Carl's mood switching, denial of the facts and total inability to take responsibility for any problem they had, the more she slowly realized that he had deep rooted psychological problems relating to women.
She read Susan Forward's book Men Who Hate Women and the Women Who Love Them .
That's when she realized that she was dating a Misogynist!

Signs of misogyny include the following, and naturally, nobody will exhibit all of these signs, but if you recognize your guy when looking at these signs, realize that you most likely cannot have a healthy happy relationship with him unless he agrees to therapy:

- Thinks his masculinity depends on dominating women
- Controls women by destroying their self-confidence
- Needs to insure that women are always less powerful than he
- Intimidates women by constantly finding fault with them
- Humiliates women in public and devalues their opinions
- Must ALWAYS win in a discussion with or about women – all encounters with or about women are seen as a battle to be won
- Blames women for failings that are in no way related to them
- Blames women for his own failings and shortcomings (or the failings and shortcomings of other men)
- Denies women's feelings and makes them wrong for feeling them
- Makes jokes or derogatory comments about women and then ridicules any woman who gets offended or upset
- Belittles or ignores women's accomplishments
- Wants to punish any woman who displeases him
- Has no remorse or guilt for the pain he causes women
- Tries to keep women from doing things they are qualified to do
- Selectively quotes authorities to substantiate his views and positions on women
- Will confuse issues by changing the subject, denial, word jugglery, lying, twisting the facts or acting as if nothing happened (when you both know that it did)
- A knight in shining armor – zeroes in on a woman to "save"
- Extremely possessive, wants all of your time and undivided attention
- Obsessively jealous, even of your women friends. Wants you to account for any time spent away from him
- Is preoccupied with sex and is sexually controlling
- Has grandiose behavior; cocky and self-centered
- Has first class spending habits; always wanting more
- Can't stand criticism; always on the defense
- He has problems with authority figures in general and women in authority in particular
- Is nasty behind the wheel and feels that other drivers' mistakes are directed toward him personally
- Has a Jekyll and Hyde personality - Nice to you in public, but cuts you down in private

- Always the victim; takes no responsibility; blames others/things/circumstances for his behavior
- Overly sensitive and sulking when he does not get his way
- Steals, uses people, always borrowing but never pays back
- Give gifts then demands favors
- Professes religious beliefs then attacks your religious beliefs

It is impossible to find happiness with this one.
He is trigger happy. Stay OUT of his range!

Chapter Fifteen

The Master of the Mixed Message

The moment Sherrie encountered this sweetie pie she knew that there was going to be something between them.

Sherrie is a realtor and had arranged to meet Mike to show him an apartment he had contacted her about. Once at the apartment they connected quickly. They kind of shared a "moment".

Their eyes locked.
Mike's eyes were deep and warm and full of promise.
Both Sherrie and Mike felt something.
As they parted Sherrie handed Mike her card, not anticipating that she was about to embark on a wild ride!

That same evening Mike texted her.

At first they chatted about the property she had shown him that day, and then he asked her out for dinner.
He seemed like a lovely guy, so why not?

A true gentleman, as well as a cool dude, he arrived for their date looking groomed, smelling great, and gallantly holding open his car door for her.
Then off they went for a candlelit dinner in a romantic restaurant!

He is a successful entrepreneur, whose exploits Sherrie recalled having read about in the paper, an artist, and a self-made man who seemed confident yet modest.

They both enjoyed the evening immensely and Sherrie felt that this may be the beginning of something very nice...

The Mixed Messenger texted her frequently and called each day. He asked her out a couple of times a week, and always arrived on time, looking good.

Ever the gentleman, he always treated, and a couple of weeks in, was already bringing her thoughtful gifts.

Sherrie started to tell her friends how much she liked him, and she waited for the relationship to progress to the next stage physically... (were they boyfriend/girlfriend? It was unclear)

Sometimes Mike came over to hang out and keep her company while she worked and sometimes they went for beach walks and talked about everything and anything.

They bonded as Mike offered Sherrie his insights on single parenting, religion, business ethics, etc. The conversations were enjoyable. He had perspective, experiences and insights that she respected.

Although Mike could be a little too sensitive at times, almost girly in his reactions to the things Sherrie said, she put it off to his artistic temperament.

He spoke of the trips he would love to go on with her, and alluded to the fact that he was falling in love with her.
But, he never reached for her hand. He never kissed, or even hugged Sherrie.

She knew that he was attracted to her *that way*, because the evening texting had turned to "sexting", and their phone calls sometimes veered off into steamy phone sex.

Sherrie realized that their relationship was smokin hot from afar, but rather tepid in the flesh.

Sherrie went off on a business trip for a few days, and Mike kept her on the phone till the wee hours of the night, telling her how much he missed her and wished that she was curled up in bed spooning with him. So naturally she was super excited to see him as soon as she got home, and was looking forward to, and highly anticipating their first kiss.

But it never came.

At this point Sherrie was confused. Clearly something was holding Mike back from moving forward with her physically, yet emotionally she could feel the relationship progress. It started to feel as if she was dealing with several different personalities.
Did he have a split personality?

Sherrie began to tease him.

Which HIM will she encounter next time?
Friendly him?
Sexting him?
Phone fantasy f---king him?

Finally Sherrie decided that it was time to ask him outright what was going on with this relationship. Why was he acting more like a friend in person, and a lover from afar?
Was there an issue?
Perhaps a medical problem?

It was definitely time to have THE TALK.

At first he simply shut down. He was taken off guard and said he needed time to think before answering Sherrie. He told her that he would call her later, but let the whole day go by before he did so.
When Sherrie finally heard from him again she felt as though she had stumbled onto the set of a soap opera.

He apologized for taking so long to call her back and then hit her with:
"It is better that you forget me".
"No matter what I tell you, I will lose you and it just breaks my heart."
And finally, "I think I will go away... to Russia." (Russia??)

He didn't want to open up with the reason for his impending disappearance and Sherrie was getting truly scared now, as well as a little pissed off.

She was asking herself what the heck his problem might be.

Sherrie told him that she was owed an explanation. Even if he could not take the relationship any farther, she deserved to know what the issue was that was holding him back. After all, didn't he expect that he would eventually have to offer up some-kind of explanation as to why he can only make love to an absent partner?

"I thought we were just friends" he told her
What??
That doesn't mesh with the late night sexting!
And then after much prodding and pleading, the Bombshell:
He has Herpes!
Ahhhh...
Okay...
"Can we be friends?" he asked.
"Of course!" she answered, "we ARE friends"!

But why was he stringing her along romantically on the phone if all he wanted was a friendship?
Why didn't he either tell her about his condition at the outset or ask if she could deal with it, or just keep the two of them in The Friend Zone?

Since Mike now felt comfortable that she had accepted his physical condition, since she had not hung up the phone on him, he hit Sherrie with:
"The next time I see you, I am going to kiss you passionately"
Huh?

The mixed messages were coming at her so fast now that she was getting mental whip -lash just trying to keep up with the status changes he was lobbing her way.

Really creeped out now, Sherrie preferred to exit the "friendship "fast.

No to the Herpes kiss Master of the Mixed Message!

This gentleman's issue is a deep seated fear of intimacy, and he latched onto the STD to keep Sherrie at arm's length.

In truth lots of couples deal with this and many other issues, by, well... dealing with them! But this personality type can use a variety of excuses to pull off the same dynamic.

It could be an age difference, religious difference, logistics or any other issue.

The end result is that he uses the issue, which was present at the outset, to manipulate the progress and/or outcome of the relationship.

He may have been burnt badly by women in the past and now prefers to flirtatiously experiment with the potential of a relationship, rather that dive in and actually have one.

He kept Sherrie guessing as he tested out the friend versus lover role, but didn't have the guts to commit to either. A woman can be pulled in two opposing directions by the Master of the Mixed Message, and it is confusing and exhausting.

Always on guard against rejection, he keeps his shield of armor ever at the ready.

The Red Flags here:
If a guy doesn't slide into 1st base by the 3rd or 4th date, beware!
Something may be up... the normal healthy male will want to progress you right into at least a little feel without too much delay.
If his hands off approach with you in person are in contrast to his hot and heavy talk when on the phone then this is a signal that he is emotionally malfunctioning on some level.
If he uses terms of endearment one minute and then terms of platonic friendship the next, and creates a crazy mixed bag of mixed messages, just know that his inner conflicts rule the relationship and it is not likely to go anywhere.

He can't figure himself out so you need to be out of there pronto!

Chapter Sixteen

What to do if you have been downgraded to "friend"?

Any time a man changes your status from lover to friend, it's time to get yourself OUT of the relationship ASAP!

Remember, this is a rejection of you as someone he is sexually attracted to! It is a downgrade of your relationship status and it is an insult.

Why would you hang on and accept this?

Women must at all times project self-worth!

Accepting whatever terms a man says he wants, just to cling to him at some level, any level, communicates the message that you are desperate to be connected to him, and will settle for whatever relationship crumbs he has to offer you.

If you are looking for an exclusive monogamous loving relationship, then you must keep that goal in sight at all times and do not accept or waste time on anything that does not match up to that goal.

You do not have to exhaust your limited emotional energy reserves by engaging in "friend" interactions with a man with whom you have had, or want to have, a romantic loving relationship with, but who does not at present want that with you anymore. This is a drain on the energy needed to focus on getting out there, looking and feeling your best, and connecting with men who ARE interested in you romantically.

Do NOT waste time analyzing his inner thoughts and motives or try to project what possible beneficial outcome might ultimately result by staying friends with a man that you love and want more with.

In fact, the one and only motivation for such a man to possibly re- kindle his lost sexual attraction to you, is for him to fear that he may lose you.

If and when he realizes that you have moved on, and that other men are interested in you, and he could lose you, a sense of urgency may kick in, and he might just reevaluate his feelings towards you.

In general, a woman who hangs around waiting and hoping for friendly feelings to morph into romantic feelings is wasting her valuable time.

Any woman who is with a man who is dragging his feet about commitment, month after month, year after year, is also wasting her time, big time!

The hunter/gatherer instinct that each and every male possesses in his DNA from time immemorial is lulled into complacency by that which is easy to come by.

The male wants and needs a challenge.

The male wants and needs to work for his target (you).
He enjoys his reward only if he has had to strive to achieve it!

It is the elusive Doe peeking from behind the bramble that gets his attention, and not the road kill lying there for the taking on his street!

You want your man to feel a sense of urgency!
You want him to feel that you are valuable and desirable, and that if he doesn't step up his game, then you will be snapped up by some other lucky dude.

So please don't serve yourself up on a platter to any man by being overly available, accepting terms for a relationship that don't suit you, accepting any bad or thoughtless behaviors, or accepting no commitment from him if at least 6 months has elapsed since you began dating.

Listen to his words.

If he tells you he is not ready or that he wants to be just friends, get your game on, and get out of there!

Throw a smile on your face, (you may have to "Fake it till you make it") and make yourself available to the many worthy loving men out there in the world just waiting to meet you.

Chapter Seventeen

Trying To Straddle the Border

No relationship is as confusing as one with a Borderline Personality.

Let's take a glimpse:

Sample:

Date one - he asks "will you see me again?"

Date two – "I am vulnerable to you, do you like me? Are you interested in us being exclusive"?

Date three – "I love you. Don't blow it"

Then:

Blissful interludes, exciting travel, future plans, marriage talk, looking for apartments....interrupted bi weekly by sudden outbursts, hang ups, walk outs, and "breaks"

Gifts given and taken back

Plans made and broken

Accusations

Criticisms

Followed by loving reunion, laughter, affection...then moody silence, shunning, rejection.

If your head is spinning and you find yourself lying awake at night trying to process the highest highs and the lowest lows in your romantic history, if your relationship is marked by your partner's sudden out bursts, accusations, Jekyll and Hyde mood switches, and irrational accusations, then you are a card carrying member of an exclusive club of co- dependents bent on saving/changing your Broderline personality disordered boyfriend.

Research reveals that although it may be possible to survive such a relationship emotionally and physically intact, it takes emotional fortitude and a rock solid support system to do so.

Expect to be the brunt of his surprise attacks, and to be made to feel as though you, and not he, are the person in need of psychotherapy.

By the time he gets done with you, you might be, if you choose to stick around!

This fellow evolved into the damaged dude he is today because his childhood was marked by abandonment and/or abuse by one or both of his parents. Now forever on the alert for any hint of rejection from the current primary emotional connection in his adult life (you), he can snap in an instant at the slightest suggestion of separation or criticism.

If you happen to visit him and then innocently suggest leaving a few days earlier than planned, he may explode in anger and throw you out, while never relating his rage to your hinted at abandonment (as he perceived it). No, rather he will pick on some totally unrelated "crime" as the catalyst for his attack.

"You can't wash 3 dinner dishes???"

"You wouldn't immediately respond to my text and get up off the beach to join me in a spontaneous visit to my friend's house???"

"GET OUT OF MY HOUSE YOU IDIOT"!!

In the aftermath of such an attack, when you are struggling to keep your sanity and to understand what has just transpired, he may also chastise you for any number of past mistakes that helped bring him to the boiling point.

He will not take responsibility for his outrageous behaviors, as his ego is as fragile as glass, and he will drive your life crazy making you feel that you are always in the wrong and deserving of the worst treatment.

The reality is, it is damned hard to predict what triggers his rage, which is of course a cry of pain *at your expense.*

NO, you can't learn to live with it and NO you can't learn to walk on eggshells and hope to avoid it.

His relationships with lovers, family and friends are marked by quarrelsome erratic behavior and irrational over–reactions to minor situations that wouldn't faze a healthy balanced person in the least.

So why are you with him?

Ahh..Because he is smart, handsome, funny, witty, charming, and romantic!

He is beguiling, illusive, and dramatic, capable of making grand gestures of love and loyalty.

However, his quirky/moody actions and unpredictable reactions tell another tale entirely.

Once he feels safely ensconced in the relationship his Prince Charming façade will crack and reveal the mood switching, unreliable, disloyal and dishonest little child that is actually at the core of his true inner self.

Please don't try to save him. Save yourself and be glad you dodged a bullet.

Case history Borderline

Joy and Artie were set up by a matchmaker. By the 3rd date, Artie had professed his love to Joy and basically swept her off her feet by following her to NYC where she had joined her family for the Thanksgiving holiday.

Prior to his arrival he had gorgeous flowers sent, and then, while there, wined and dined her, charmed her family and friends, and quizzed her as to where and when she wanted to marry him.

Their first month together was like a dream. Joy realized that this was "it"! This relationship with Artie felt like the "Warm bath" her friend had used as an analogy as to how the *right* relationship should feel.

But, at the one month mark, things began to change, and would never be the same again.

From the one month mark onward, Joy found herself looking for her original boyfriend, and anguished that she could not seem to recapture him. He had been replaced by a moody and unpredictable twin who somehow found fault with every action, or inaction of Joy's. To this day, she mourns and longs for the Artie that she first met. What she had no way of knowing at the time, was that Artie was presenting a false self to Joy, and that his real self was a very damaged man unable to maintain a smooth and stable relationship, with *anyone*.

One month in:

Joy and Artie are speaking on the phone and he is expressing the idea of reporting the recent illegal actions of a very well-known and dangerous character in their community, to the authorities. Joy, scared and horrified as she imagines the probable outcome, which in her opinion would be the pummeling of her boyfriend by the fiend in question, pleads with Artie to not get involved. She tells him that if he does so, then perhaps this is a sign that they are not really "meant to be" because if he goes in the direction he is speaking of, it will not end well. She is terrified of losing Artie.

All of a sudden the phone goes dead. Joy calls Artie and asks him if he hung up on her?

He had. He hung up on her because she had the audacity to speak the words "maybe we are not meant to be".

In the ensuing weeks and months Artie embarks on a pattern of walking out on Joy, and then shunning her for days or weeks, whenever he doesn't like, or misinterprets, what she says.

This is torment for Joy.

4 months in:

They are sitting in Artie's car relaxing and listening to music, killing time until their dinner date with another couple. Joy looks at Artie lovingly and asks him how it was possible that he knew instantly upon meeting her, that she was "The One".

"How can a person *just know*, so quickly", she asks

Artie is curt and tells her not to nag him.

"Why can't we just relax and enjoy the moment" he asks. "

Why do you have to nag me!!?"

The next day Joy is relaxing on the beach after work when a text comes from Artie. He sends her an unfamiliar address and says "I am here". Since Joy had not heard from him since last night when he coldly told her not to nag him, she isn't sure what to do or what Artie had in mind. She responds "have a nice time".

Later that evening Artie informs her that he is cancelling the plans they had made to spend the weekend together because she did not show up to the address he had sent her. How was she supposed to know that his text was a request for her to join him at the address he sent her?? Artie was now not talking to her. In effect, he was punishing her.

5 months in:

Joy and Artie are strolling down the path back to their bungalow after a lovely dinner at the posh tropical Island resort they were staying at for a week long holiday over Easter Break. Joy decides now may be a good time to voice her concern over what she perceived was a possible health issue with Artie.

"Honey"... she starts

"I am thinking that maybe when we get back you should go for a physical and some blood tests because I see that you want to spend so much time resting in the hotel room in the dark, instead of enjoying the pool and the beach with me. Maybe it's not normal that you are so tired all the time. I'm worried about you".

Artie explains that he doesn't believe in physicals, there is nothing wrong with him, and moreover, why should Joy assume that resting a lot is a sign of a medical problem? What about those eastern cultures that encourage restful meditation? It is a crazy American miss -perception that "Normal" means active and engaging!

Artie then spirals into a rage telling Joy to "leave me alone!"

He becomes sullen and distant until Joy apologizes for proffering her opinion.

8 months in:

They are staying in Artie's home in Europe, and Artie has just picked up Joy from the airport after her 3 day visit to a friend in London who had just lost her father. He asks her if he should pick up some fresh fish for her to prepare for them for dinner. Joy tells Artie that she is simply too exhausted and drained to cook, and that she still has to get onto her computer and check in with work.

Can they go to a restaurant for a quick bite she asks?

Artie does not want to go to a restaurant, but is willing to go and pick up some ready-made food and bring it home for dinner.

Joy gets onto her computer and tries to catch up on her missed work.

When Artie arrives home with the food, she reaches for the paper plates, but Artie is arching his eyebrow in surprise at that choice, and insists on using the fine China.

After the meal, Joy, who is now longing to get into bed and is too tired to even take her customary evening shower, asks Artie if he could please deal with the dishes. She tells him she is sooo tired, but she would like to enter a clean kitchen tomorrow morning and whip up a nice meal for them.
Then she lies on her bed and is about to fall asleep in her clothing, when Artie comes in to chat.

Joy expresses to Artie that she may want to cut her 4 week trip to Europe with him by one week, so as to spend time with her family back in the States.

Artie says "no that is not acceptable".

He sits on the foot of the bed and tells her that in her absence, he realized that he is better off living without someone who worries, and Joy has worries.

Joy feels an impending sense of doom... due to his gloom.

The next morning she awakes early and gets right back onto her computer to check into her mounting work load.

Artie comes down, makes coffee and approaches Joy. He is now in "attack mode"

He gets in her face as he shouts "Why couldn't you wash the dinner dishes!!!! Shocked, she stammers that she had been too tired, why couldn't he have done it?

"You don't tell a man to do that!!!" he screams

"You should leave!!" He tells her to "Just go"

Joy is totally thrown off guard. Artie has just told her to leave today! She asks if the return date on her ticket can be modified and he yells "NO"!

Then he turns his back and proceeds to head off to the local café to meet his friends.

Joy pleads with him to stay and talk this out with her, to no avail.

So, shaking and crying Joy calls the airline, discovers that she can change her return ticket with a change fee, and arranges to leave the next day.

Artie returns from the café and behaves as if nothing has happened.

Would she like to go for coffee with him?

"Artie, you have told me to leave and so I arranged a ticket to go back to the States tomorrow".

"You are sick!" Artie screams at her, pointing his finger at her face. "I never said that! You imagined it"

"But Artie, you told me to go, and I asked if I could change my return flight, and you said no, but I inquired with the airline and I was able to change it with a fee!"

"GET OUT OF MY HOUSE" Artie screams slamming his fist on the table.

"YOU ARE AN IDIOT"

In pure shock Joy again calls the airline and now arranges an immediate flight out of there.

She gathers her things, throws them into her suitcases and leaves town.

Arriving in NY she collapses into the arms of her family and lies in bed for two weeks trying to recover and to make sense of what she has just experienced.

It took six months, a lot of research, and the advice of a good therapist to discover the problem. Artie is a Borderline personality.

He was thrown into rage/rejection mode by the merest hint that Joy may want to cut her visit short by a week, combined with her refusal to wash the dinner dishes, which he interpreted as distancing behavior on her part.

In a relationship with a Borderline individual, the initial "honeymoon" period will devolve into a series of break ups and make ups with the non-Borderline struggling to understand what sets her partner off.

The Borderline personality is known for "splitting" which means that he is either idolizing his girlfriend, or vilifying her.

When she does anything that he interprets as annoying, abandoning, rejecting, or critical, he will turn his back on her, casting her into the abyss.

When he is pleased with her, he is the ideal loving and caring partner making future plans and showing up with gifts.

His switching can happen in a flash.

The Borderline personality is not easily recognized early in a relationship as he is in "get the girl" mode, and therefore on his best behavior. The Red Flags appear only after the emotional tie is established, and the female has now become his primary emotional attachment. This attachment induces a subconscious fear in the borderline male.

Will she leave him?

Will she devalue him as his mother and /or father did?

His rage is simmering under the surface and about to spring forth at any time.

Is there hope for him?

Yes!

Studies show that the Borderline personality can successfully be treated and can respond well to certain therapies. The trick is to get them into therapy, as they typically believe that they are the victims. Everyone else is in the wrong except them!

So what are the Red Flags here?

Be on the lookout for the "too much too soon" aspect.

If he is prodding you along towards commitment almost from the outset, if he is madly in love by date 4 – these are **Red Flags**.

If he is quarrelsome with people in general and expresses the notion that others are against him and that he is a misunderstood victim... watchhit!!

If he uses shunning as a means to punish you for something you expressed, or did
If he never says he is sorry, but pins all problems and misunderstandings on you

If his mood switches suddenly to the point that you want to nickname him Dr. Jekyll and Mr. Hyde.
If you perceive that he doesn't have any close friendships
If his reputation around town is that people are fearful of him
If he does not have happy relationships with his family members

Obviously one or two of these signs are not a strong indicator of a problem, but if your guy displays several, or all of these "symptoms", you must be very cautious about proceeding with the relationship.
Be warned.
Without therapy, there is no happy ending possible here.

Chapter Eighteen

Commitment Phobia

The dreaded commitment phobic guy will make you crazy as he reels you in and out like a fish on the line.

Due to his fears of making a commitment, he will most likely throw you back in the pond if you get too close.

His fears rule and direct the course of the relationship, though he is usually not conscious of this fact.

Count on not being able to count on him.

Count on him sabotaging important dates such as birthdays and anniversaries.

He may do this by forgetting them, downplaying them, or avoiding addressing them.

"The Unavailable Dream Boat", the "Passive Pot Head" and Mr. Quick Turnaround are examples of commitment phobic men who will string you along ad infinitum.

Just when the relationship feels warm and cozy, safe and secure to you, he will find it boring, suffocating and unsafe. As such he will move to undermine whatever you have had going for you.

The reason?

His fears of emotional intimacy are stronger than his desire for a stable, exclusive, committed relationship. He is grappling with inner conflict. A part of him sincerely wants to be in a committed relationship. A part of him is terrified that you will abandon him, hurt him, reject him, deceive him, cheat on him, use him, demean him or emasculate him.

The commitment phobic person is reacting to a trauma in his history.

It is not always easy to recognize commitment phobia early on. He may come on strong and appear to be everything you ever wanted in a man.

In his pursuit phase, he will be doing everything to please and impress you. In this phase he will jump through hoops to make you his. It is only when he finally succeeds, that he begins to reveal the Red Flags of the commitment phobic man.

The frequency of his contact will start to drop off. He will become distant and detached. He may neglect to introduce you to his friends and acquaintances, should you bump into them when out together. He will show little or no interest in making plans for anything in the future. Your intimate life may fizzle...

The more you attempt to fill the void in the relationship by doing and being more for him, the more he pulls back, until he disappears. Usually with no warning or logical explanation.

In the worst case scenarios, you may get engaged to him, give up your apartment to move into his, and leave your job so that you can live in his city, and then find yourself left at the altar!

Note that a Commitment Phobic man who gets married STILL has commitment issues.

These issues may surface in the marriage in the following ways:
He will:
"Forget" anniversaries and/or birthdays or any other important milestone
Pull back sexually
Cheat
Come home late or not at all
Gamble
Drink
Have angry outbursts
In short he will express his inner conflict by "acting out" in very hurtful ways.
Don't think the problem ends with **"I do"**.

It's better if **you don't!**

Chapter Nineteen

The Detached Loner

This wonder boy doesn't seem to need much in the way of human companionship, and in fact, tries to avoid it whenever possible!

Here is a real life example:

Though not a "people person", David works as a therapist, an irony that does not go unnoticed as he fumbles his way through any contact with his peers.

He is a highly intelligent and well educated professional, soft spoken and polite.

In the cultural circle he comes from, he stands out like a sore thumb.

While they are merchants, wheeling and dealing in the world of buying and selling jewelry, furniture, carpets and real estate, he has chosen a different path and is a highly trained clinical psychologist.

While his family and friends love to come together, eating and drinking with gusto, teasing each other and arguing, laughing and taking pleasure in each other's company whenever possible, he is always a bit removed from the action.

Though he enjoys being with his family, he doesn't like to socialize, is uncomfortable in a crowd, and will avoid a large group or party scene at all costs.

His parents are the matriarch and patriarch of a large clan. They are respected by all and are often asked to dispense advice as well as financial backing. He does not feel comfortable approaching them for either, and prefers to wing it on his own.

Rose has always loved to socialize, is a people person and an emotional, giving soul.

Why on earth was she attracted to him?

David has sought her out because it's time that he finds himself a wife.

Rose is very pretty, and is outside the mainstream of his culture.

David is secretly hoping that Rose will not mind being kept at emotional arm's length for the rest of her life.

In his culture, one marries within their own tightly knit community. Outsiders are discouraged from marrying into their group. He knows all this, yet David chooses to pursue Rose!

Thus he is rebelling, at her expense.

What would the impact on Rose be?

She is considered an outsider to his family and friends. She is not what they expected him to bring home.

They feign acceptance of Rose, but grumble under their breath, wondering why he didn't marry a girl from their group.

David had been engaged to marry a girl from his community, but he wasn't really into her, let the engagement fizzle, and was left at loose ends.

Eventually he heard about the pretty "out of towner" and opted to check Rose out. Maybe it was his silent rebellion against all that was familiar to him. Maybe it was his way of declaring his independence in a family where loyalty and cohesion to the community is the status quo.

But the result is, he has managed to get Rose to settle for living on the fringe, as he does.

As a new young couple just starting out in life together, there isn't much time to notice the disparity. The babies are coming one after another and it's all they can do to keep their heads above water.

It's not long before Rose starts to feel the pain of the emotional distance that David seems to need to maintain between them, as well as everyone else in the world. Rose longs to connect, but David has no such need.

His work keeps him away from home for long hours each day. They fall into a pattern of Rose never expecting him home for dinner with the family. They never go on a "date night", or to the movies, or restaurants, and only rarely go on a vacation.

He is not much of a go-getter, not really motivated, and doesn't earn much. David expects Rose to work full time, and to pay for the kid's private school tuition as well as most of the household expenses and any luxuries she might yearn for.

David doesn't validate what Rose does for him, and his family doesn't seem to appreciate her or even see her as an individual with needs and desires of her own.

After making their babies, their intimate life fizzles out as David is no longer interested in physical contact. Rose is left feeling all alone in life and feeling that she may as well be single.

The detached loner is not partner material and will not make a good husband or boyfriend

It is vital that women notice the signs of a potential detached loner right from the get go, and not try to kid herself that he is just "shy" or "inhibited" .

What he is is dysfunctional.

In fact, he may suffer from Schizoid personality disorder, which is character-ized by the preference for being alone in the following ways:

He doesn't enjoy family life or close relationships.
He might tolerate them, or understand why others in his family need them, but he doesn't get much enjoyment out of them himself.
Given the choice, he prefers to do something alone.
There aren't many things he likes to do.
He does not have any close friends.

He doesn't really care much what other people think about him.
He doesn't show emotion.

Please consider the above cluster to be significant Red Flags!

Leave the loner to his own devices and skedaddle!

Chapter Twenty

Red Flag Man – Mama's Boy

The Mama's boy is that guy who is quite obviously over- involved with his mom.

A telling sign of mental health in a man is independent living with healthy levels of family contact and interaction.

It is healthy if he makes his *own decisions.*

It is unhealthy if he has a compulsion to consult with Mom before making basic life choices such as "what shall I order for lunch?" "Where shall I go on vacation?" or "shall I continue to date this girl?"

While it is admirable when a man is respectful and considerate of his mom (and all of his family members), it is another matter entirely if he is overly connected to and compelled to include his mother or consult with his mother, in his daily life. It is a RED FLAG if he takes it to the extreme by including his mom in his dates, allowing his mom to interfere with his relationship or sharing details of his intimate, private life with her.

Can your boyfriend make an important purchase or decision without consulting his mother?
Does his mother wind up sometimes coming along on your dates?
Does he discuss the intimate details of your relationship with his mom?
Does his mom have a green light to drop in on him/you two, unannounced?
Does he compare you to his mom?
Does he mention or compare his mom's style of dressing, cooking, working out, etc?
Is he capable of committing to you despite the fact that you may not represent his mother's ideal choice of a mate for him?

A man who has not been able to coast along without the constant interference, approval and consultation with his mother will not make a good husband or boyfriend in the long term.

The primary focus of a boyfriend or husband is supposed to be on his *partner, not on pleasing his mother*.

It is important that an adult partner is one who has *launched*. Visiting the nest occasionally is fine but running back to it or constantly seeking guidance from his parents is an indication that he is not fully functional as an adult. Most importantly it shows that he is not capable of running his own household or heading up his own family, as he lacks the self confidence to do so.

If your boyfriend wants to bring his mom along on some of your dates, live with or in very close proximity to his mom, regularly prioritize his mom's needs and desires over yours, this is a big RED FLAG.

If this is the current situation, it is more likely than not to remain that way.

YOU are not going to change this dynamic.

Change comes from within a person and not from the pressure or demands of another. Even if he agrees to change the dynamic in order to keep you around, the change is unlikely to last unless he goes for therapy, and even then, there can be no guarantee.

The old adage "What you see is what you get" should be kept in mind if you are involved with a Mama's boy.

Don't accept second place. If he is a Mama's boy, leave with grace.

Chapter Twenty-One

Red Flag Man – Rebounding Romancer

He is wooing you a mile a minute, sweeping you off your feet so fast you don't know what hit you. He is a storm of emotion coming at you, lifting you off your feet into Lala land!

Until you have connected the dots, (in the aftermath) you will not know that the power that is feeding this emotional vortex is his desperate urge to fill the terrible void in his life.

You meet and are charmed by his good looks and sensitivity. He is easy going, fun to be around and, unlike most guys you've met, he appears to be emotionally available and easy to connect with.

He has just been through a painful break up, and he opens his heart to you, sharing his feelings of disappointment, anger and guilt. You listen patiently and offer him words of comfort, support, and insight.

Though initially you were not incredibly attracted to him, and maintained your emotional space, preferring to keep him at arm's length, soon enough you find that he has broken down your walls.

You fall head over heels in love with him.

You enjoy great times together! You have a lot in common and enjoy spending weekends going for long walks, antiquing, hanging out at his place.

Your connection is hot and passionate.

The two of you spend hours in deep conversation, which are mostly centered on exploring what might have gone wrong with his recent failed marriage. What might he or his wife have done differently? Were the two of them ever right for each other? What about the impact on his little boy?

You patiently console him, all the while believing that in doing so, you are creating the foundations of your own, more successful relationship with each other.

What bugs you is that he does not seem to make you a priority in his life. You are feeling more like filler.

Plans or not, if his kid calls and wants to come over, he wants you outta there in 10 minutes flat!

When you confront him on it later, he acknowledges how insensitive he was and apologizes profusely. Of course he should have handled it differently, he confesses!

He should have given you at least 30 minutes, instead of only 10, to hi -tail it out of there before his kid arrived!

Though your conversations are deep, connected and meaningful and the times you spend together are wonderful, you can't help but feel that he is not fully present in the relationship.

He is capable of casting your plans aside in a flash, if he receives a call from his ex, or his kid, asking him to help them with something, or to join in on something. He chooses not to work around his plans with you, and will abandon you easily if confronted with the opportunity to play the role of "involved dad" or "still caring ex-husband"

You are confused and unable to reconcile the wild and passionate night before, with this morning's easy dismissal.

"Hey, my son will be here with his mom in 10 minutes so I think you better get dressed and get going. Catch ya later!"

Often he calls to invite you over when he has his son with him for the weekend.

Happily you bound on over and enjoy preparing dinner, playing games and bonding. However, you notice that when he has a free night, he will opt to go practice with his band, rather than spend time with you.

Annoying as it is, you put up with this because you are of the belief that all that you have shared, and gone through together, including the frustrations, are actually the building blocks of your own rock solid future.

You are certain that as soon as his divorce is finalized, you two will be creating your own life together, which will be happier and more fulfilling for him that the broken down relationship he is now in the process of exiting.

So you wait it out.

You put up with his occasional dismissive behaviors.

And finally, the moment you have been waiting for! He is divorced! Free to move forward with you!

And then....

He is GONE

You so generously supported and guided him through the toughest emotional time of his life! And now...

He has left you on the driveway like a wrench.

Yes, you were a tool. The tool he needed to extricate himself from his failed marriage, and now he is ready to seek out his next prospect.

Rebound relationships are almost certainly doomed to fail.

A man *in the process* of a break up is not emotionally available to construct his next relationship.

He is only available for using you to segue out of his emotional morass.

Do not allow yourself to be the tool a man needs to bust out of his marriage.

Keep away from rebound romance.

You will know the Red Flags with this one.

He is going through, or has just gone through a break up

He is still processing it and he wants to talk about it incessantly

You are not his priority

If the above factors are all present, then this is a **Red Flag Man**

He will not Morph into the committed loving partner you are fantasizing about

Chapter Twenty-Two

Red Flag Man – Mr. Quick Turnaround

To his credit, Mr. Quick does not drag your heart over the coals before revealing his emotional shackles.

Yes he comes on strong as do many of our RF men, but he will not dangle you on the line for long.

This is a man of integrity who recognizes that his fears and issues rule his heart.

It's a bummer because he can be a real charmer.

Eyes sparkling with warmth and depth

Gallantry

Sophistication

Charm

Intelligent, successful and accomplished, one would expect Mr. Quick to be brimming with self-confidence, and ready to forge ahead with any lady who peeks his interest.

At first, he seems to do just that. He will chat amicably, flirt, even dance the night away with her.

He may follow up on a first encounter with a flurry of flattering emails hinting at a romance in the offing. This behavior will last only until the moment that Mr. Quick senses that his flirtations are drawing in the subject.

Her positive response will activate his disengagement mode immediately. Proclaiming an interest in nothing more than friendship, the flirtations will cease, and the ensuing communications may evolve into an analysis of his inner demons, past hurts and resulting fears.

Mr. Quick Turn Around has experienced disappointment in love, and will posit that Fear Triumphs over Love.

The irony is that all the insights and intuitions he may have for other people's strengths and weaknesses do not extend to the man in the mirror.
Though he knows he is blocked, he can't explain why he pursues a solitary life path.

Do not try to convince him to change his mind. Just walk away with your pride intact. This guy aint committing to anyone!

Chapter Twenty-Three

Rich But Cheap Status Seeker

We all know that you can't buy class, but some hope to marry it, believing that they will achieve the status that has thus far eluded them.

Face it, there are some pretty scrungy characters out there, and some of them have had great financial success. They may be dogs but they've got the big bucks and hope to use them to rein in a classy girl.

Here's a true life example:

Jerry was a pretty slick slum lord. As he walked around his neighborhood he ran into lots of people he knew, most of whom had an ax to grind with him. He'd been lording it over his government subsidized tenants, bullying them as he collected his rent, with a clear conscience as well as a sense of self satisfaction.

He had risen above his childhood circumstances, made it big on his own, but remained mired in the murk of his past.

His parents raised him in a shabby environment. It was the opposite of luxurious, (though money was not an issue!)

They lived below the frugal level and horded their money and possessions. Jerry grew up having been taught that money was to be made, but not spent on anything but the bare essentials, and now he wanted to rise above all that and learn how to live the good life.

Jerry wanted to make a new independent life with a classy wife, and knew that he would have to rely on her to show him the way.

One day his sister introduced him to her former class mate, Risa, who just happened to be his idea of the perfect girl.

Risa had been raised by wealthy parents, with live- in domestic help, in a sophisticated international environment. Risa's parents collected art and antiques as they traveled the world for business, returning home from time to time to check in on her and her siblings. She had mixed with high society, was educated, worldly and beautifully dressed. Risa was down to earth and not at all snobby, despite having always enjoyed the best of everything. Her parents had taught her a work ethic, and she worked hard at her profession, taking pride in her accomplishments.

When Risa's class mate suggested introducing her to her brother, she was initially not really interested. She already had a boyfriend she was into, but to be polite, Risa agreed to meet him as a friend.

From the first glance she felt that this guy was not at all her type.

Oh he had tried to class up his act!

With a wad of dough in his pocket, his hair slicked back and a diamond pinky ring on his finger, he would saunter into the finest restaurant; tip the maître d for the best table in the house, and order up the most expensive menu options, all in an effort to impress Risa.

And impress her it did!

Jerry stared deeply into Risa's eyes as they talked about everything, including her boyfriend.

Mr. Status Seeker is a patient guy and his game was ON!

Jerry became the caring friend who wanted to be there for Risa as she expressed her doubts and insecurities. He was there when she needed him to open up to, or help her out with the business she was trying to get off the ground.

Risa would offer to split the tab in the restaurant, and he always accepted. Jerry sent his assistant to help Risa set up her new office, and when she offered him a $20 tip to pass on to the assistant, he accepted it.

She didn't mind too much because the understanding was that they were just friends...she and Jerry were not a couple.

The more Risa's romantic relationship with her boyfriend faltered the more vulnerable she become to Jerry, aka Mr. Cheap Rich Status Seeker. He seemed to appreciate her and to desire her company much more than her boyfriend did. Jerry made sure to deride and criticize her boyfriend whenever she poured out your heart to him on a "friend date."

Jerry eventually melted Risa with that gaze of his and she finally began to succumb to his charms as he assured her that HE would never let her down the way the BF did...HE would always be there for her... HE would always take care of her...

Risa began to think "maybe this dude is cooler than I gave him credit for..." BOOM! - THE moment Jerry had been waiting for had arrived!

Risa's defenses had come down, and Jerry's game plan moved into high gear. What Risa didn't yet know is that at the end of his day, after he collected the rent from the tenants of the government subsidized housing projects he owned and operated, he returned to his sparsely furnished studio apartment with nothing more than a mattress to sleep on.

Jerry didn't need much.

He was raised by simple folk in an environment that bellied their actual financial circumstances. For even though they were richer than G-d, they opted to live in a cluttered run down dump. In fact it was so bad, that Mr. Cheap Rich Status Seeker would not bring his new girl home to his folks, as he would never want her to see how they live.

Though their two backgrounds could not be more different, there was something intriguing about Jerry that Risa was drawn to. He claimed he wanted to protect her. He wanted to be her ROCK and he told her that he would provide whatever she needed.

Once they became an item, Jerry started to bring Risa on his gambling jaunts to Las Vegas and Atlantic City!

He turned out to be a real operator... He was a high roller raking in the chips, while the hotel was comping everything for the two of them! He played and played the weekends away and eventually Risa came to realize that this is was his idea of a working vacation.

He had also figured out a way to beat the system.

When Jerry won at the slot machines and crap tables he got compted by the hotel, and when he lost he also got compted. He made a point to always be either a big winner or loser, by surreptitiously passing on his excess chips to Risa, so she could go and cash them out while he appeared to be losing.

Now they were partners in crime.

He collected a mountain of cash and Risa found it sexy and scary at the same time...

Before she knew it he was pressuring her to get married, right away. He offered Risa a big diamond and a flashy lifestyle, but she was not into it at all because she is low key by nature and not interested in the baubles he dangled before her.

At this point, all Risa wanted was him, and a normal safe secure life home life together.

When Jerry tasked Risa with finding a Townhouse in the city... or a mansion in the burbs, it was exciting! She made it her project to find some great deals on townhouses and mansions... but somehow, none of them were "good enough". He made halfhearted absurdly low offers and she began to wonder what he was thinking! He suggested that for now, they should move back to Queens, where he grew up, and she good naturedly agreed.

Once they married it started to become apparent that the "temporary" tenement apartment they were living in was gonna be as good as it gets, and though he talked a good game in the pursuit phase, his wallet was clamped shut now that he had her.

In fact it started to feel as if Risa had missed her opportunity to get anything at all from him, when she had shown a lack of interest in accepting that diamond ring.

Soon enough his desire turned to distain.

The promises and plans turned to pulp.

As Risa began to express dissatisfaction with the circumstances, Jerry became angrier and angrier. Even the basics become an issue as he refused to buy her a car and even got a bit rough with her physically when they argued.

What happened here?

Why was Mr. Cheap Rich Status Seeker willing to spend the big bucks to impress Risa when she was his girlfriend, but then withheld grocery money from her as his wife??

This type of guy is trying so hard to change his station in life, but isn't able do it alone.

He needs a classy partner to latch onto who can raise him up out of the gutter.

The key is timing.

The minute the two of them switched out of friend and into romance gear, the window of opportunity opened. Jerry *needed* Risa to inspire him to go after the things she wanted right from the get- go.

He was attracted to her like a moth to a flame, but lost his way when she dimmed her lights.

How did she dim them?

By being too accommodating!

No needs!

Not much interested in the mansion or the diamond necklace, she gave him nothing to strive for. He soon lost respect for the one he originally looked up to to raise his standards.

All males are programmed to hunt and gather and most get a great deal of satisfaction in *providing*.

The game changer with this type of guy is that his low self-esteem was not triggered into high, when Risa refused to let him strive for the big ticket items. He thought he had bought himself a 1st class ticket into society and was dismayed to discover she was happier in coach.

As a result he has lost both his respect and attraction to Risa as she failed to serve his original purpose. In fact, by being so low maintenance, she reminded him of his mom!

The last thing he needed was to feel pulled back to his ratty roots.
All guys subconsciously resonate with a girl who gives off Mom vibes, and that explains some of the initial attraction. In his case, he was hoping that Risa would be the motivator he never had.

Resentful that he wound up with a woman who needed so little, that he may as well have stayed single, he burns with rage and withholds even bare essentials.

A marriage of this nature of course cannot last long as the couple's objectives are too divergent.

What were the red flags flapping on Mr. Cheap/Rich Status Seeker's pole?

(Beware the pinky ring!)

He was a bit too enthusiastic when Risa offered to split the bill on their "just friends" dinner date.

He lured her with talk of fancy real estate but lived in a crappy apartment. Their backgrounds were way too different and their agendas totally differed as well.

His dishonest wheeling dealing should have been a deal breaker!

She sought a safe secure marriage with a loving stable husband and he wanted a girl with a sense of entitlement who would push him to provide the best of everything.

Once Risa agreed to move back to the other side of the tracks, he quickly shed his nice guy routine and became frustrated, angry and violent in the absence of pressure to perform.

THE RED FLAG MAN

How did he become like this?

He was always lacking a proper role model.

He was taught to try to get something for nothing, and to use everything he got to his advantage.

He saw the discrepancy between the resources he had access to, and the life style his family lived, but he didn't know how to resolve it alone.
Inside he feels empty, insecure and even self-loathing

Avoid cheesy guys with pinky rings!

Mr. Cheap Rich Status Seeker showed textbook signs of insecurity:

Insecurity may contribute to the development of shyness, paranoia and social withdrawal, or alternatively it may encourage compensatory behaviors such as arrogance, aggression, or bullying, in some cases.

He was also controlling.

Note to self - You are not a stepping stone to high society for use by a low class guy!

Chapter Twenty-Four

Cultural/Religious Differences: The Wanna be Monk

Jane is an all American girl from a Waspy Quaker family in Delaware.

In College, she met Anil, a Tibetan whose family lives in exile in India.

The couple fell deeply in love.

After college, Jane and Anil couldn't bear to be parted, so they decided that Jane should return to India with him.

Anil's family lives in a community of Tibetan exiles, and practices strict Buddhism. In fact, Anil's dad used to be the Dahlia Lama's right hand man, and once held aspirations of becoming a monk. However, he gave up his dream of celibacy when he fell in love with Anil's mom, an American beauty who grew up in France and converted to Buddhism.

The family dream for Anil has always been that he become the Tibetan Monk his father should have been. Needless to say, they were less than thrilled when he came home with a non-Buddhist American girl friend. They do not accept Jane as one of their tribe, but rather just put up with her.

The family is in the business of Tibetan handmade crafts, and language instruction.

Anil and Jane live together in his boyhood room in the family home, and Jane spends her days teaching English and weaving yak wool into Tibetan caftans for the family biz.

As it is considered highly inappropriate in this culture for an unmarried couple to live together, Anil and Jane have been pretending to the public that they are married.

This has been going on for 6 years, and all involved have fallen into a routine.

The problem is that Jane's heart's desire is to be Anil's proper wife, not just a pretend version. She longs to hold her head high, bring him home to her folks and face the world together as man and wife. She wants to have a home of her own and start a family.

Her sacrifices have been great.

She has left the country, culture and religion that she grew up in, and traveled to the other side of the world, to live with an unwelcoming and non-accepting family.

Anil has not had to adapt to anything at all, but has merely slipped her into his world, with neither the promise nor hint that she will ever be anything more to him than his roommate in his parents' home.

Moreover, as his role as sacrificial lamb for his family is pretty heavy to bear, he spends most of his time chilled out on weed.

Stoned out in his bedroom with his American girlfriend, he avoids fulfilling both the family expectations that he become a monk, and Jane's expectations that he become her husband.

He is stuck.

No woman should put her personal gratification, family or ambitions aside, for those of a man.

Her value to him plummets when he perceives that she is willing to do so.

No woman should have the expectation that a situation which has gone on for years, will suddenly change.

Status quo is all he can offer her.

This girl needs to go home now!

What she fails to see is that the more she adapts herself to the needs and desires of her wanna be monk boyfriend, the less valued she is by him and his family. She has subjugated her needs to his, and deludes herself, thinking that eventually Anil will break away from family tradition and marry her.

She refuses to acknowledge the reality that his cultural ties and obligations are more powerful than his desire to please her.

Until she separates herself from this no-win situation she will remain in a stagnant pile of yak hair.

Ladies, please try to resist the pull of a man from a foreign culture. There **will be only frustration** as expectations continually fail to be met on both sides.

Chapter Twenty-Five

So What *Should* you do?
What should you *not do*?

We have gone over the various warning signs of a Red Flag Man as well as the reasons it is important to take those signs seriously.

So now you know *who not to date*.

Now I would like to give you an overview of *what not to do* when dating.

Even when we are lucky enough to find a really great guy, if we mishandle the initial moments of our relationship we can turn him off and sour the whole thing.

To get things off to the right start, it is quite important to **always** project self confidence, **self worth** and **emotional independence.**

I cannot stress this enough (as all of you who have been following my Red Flag Man Blogs know!).

From time immemorial, men have been wired to go out there and face the challenge of the chase in an effort to acquire what they need for the survival of themselves and their families. That means that their very DNA is designed to give men the desire to work for what they need and want, as well as to seek out quality goods.

Times change. Human nature does not.

Though guys today may not be seeking out women with physical prowess or the ability to gather berries and skin a bison, it is still true that men are most attracted to women who appear to be self confident and self sufficient emotionally.

Therefore, when trying to attract and keep a partner, project self-worth first and foremost.

How do we do this?

We do this by letting our guy know that we have a full, busy and fulfilling life. We do not want him to think that we are checking our phone every 5 seconds for a communication from him. We don't ever want him to think we are stalking his social media!

Here is my list of DON'TS:

Don't ask a guy out or suggest what to do on a date unless he asks you to suggest something.

Don't buy him presents before he has bought you a present

Don't agree to go out with him at the very last minute, as though your life revolves around him and you have just been sitting around waiting for him to ask you out.

Don't introduce him to your significant people until you have been dating at least a few months.

Never accept rude or selfish behavior.

We do not make any man the center of our existence.

Don't call or text him (unless you are well into a committed relationship)

The reason that it is unwise for a woman to initiate contact with a man, to suggest date ideas or to buy him presents is that by doing so you deprive him of the very thing that excites him the most – the pursuit! As mentioned, a man is wired to go out there and get what he needs and wants.

If we assume the masculine role by asking him out or reaching out to him by phone or message, or by surprising him with a gift, then we are *placing him* in the role of the pursued, rather than the pursuer. While this may work to get you a date or a few dates, it will eventually back fire because deep inside men are turned on by the challenge of the pursuit. He wants to work to get you. He appreciates you when he has worked to win you over. When he has invested time, emotion and money into making you his, then he treasures you.

If he is pushed by you into going out and treated by you to presents, sex, or the honor of meeting your closest people right away, then he ultimately resents your desire to spend time with him!

He feels trapped.

He does not value a woman who takes measures to win him over.

A man truly enjoys the work he puts into winning your heart.

When a woman is elusive, seemingly hard to get, preoccupied with other endeavors, the man is driven to distraction just trying to dream up ways to get her attention and to capture her heart.

Likewise, when he asks to see you last minute and you agree, the message you are sending is that you are not high value. You are too available. There is no sense of urgency for him to plan a date or to do anything at all to win you over because when he wants to see you on a moment's notice – poof! He has you! All the work he so loves to do to get his girl has vanished.

You are not high value, but easily gotten cheap goods.

What happens when we do not follow the above advice? If a woman thinks she "knows better" or "knows him better" and she agrees to a request for a last minute date, or worse, initiates a date, the man may well agree. A relationship may even develop. Even a marriage may result eventually. However, the relationship will not be as healthy or satisfying as one in which the man gets to play the role he is wired to play.

As an example, how do we women treat the $1000 designer shoes we saved up to purchase? We are excited to finally have them! We appreciate the work we put in to earn the money to make that purchase! So we lovingly give them a place of honor on our closet shelf and fantasize about when and where we will get to wear them and even to show them off.

However, when we are able to acquire those same shoes at a sample sale for $50, they will most likely end up tumbling around our closet floor, often forgotten.

Human nature is to value that which we must work to achieve or to acquire, and this drive is even more pronounced in the males of our species for the specific reason that it was traditionally always the role of a male to hunt and gather and provide for his woman and their children. It is an ancient but unchanging fact of life, no matter how much modern times and work ethics may change.

Women are care takers by nature.

They want to nurture, show love and do thoughtful things for the people they love.
HOWEVER, *before engagement and marriage,* it is **not** a good idea to be too giving, do too much, be too available or show that you care *too much.*
Is this cruel?
NO!
In order to attract and keep the man she is crazy about, a woman must stay in her **feminine zone.**
In the feminine zone a woman is the receiver of attention, gifts and affection and *she is looking to the man to suggest and make the dates and plans for them as a couple.*

She is busy and happy with her own life, is not available every time he snaps his fingers, and is also not an open book spilling her guts over every detail of her life.

She does not regale her man with the nifty gritty of her past relationships or financial problems or family struggles.
She is never a "Debbie Downer". Rather she is happy and upbeat and preoccupied with all of the fun and magical things she has going on in her own life.

A woman should not buy gifts, send love notes, arrange theater tickets, or suggest dates with the man she is seeing.
All of that is the domain of the male.

It is he who must drive the relationship forward and it is he who, in his effort to win her heart, must think of how to demonstrate his desire for her.
HE is the one who should be dreaming up fun dates, buying her thoughtful gifts and cards and basically "working" to attract her, and to earn her love.

If you have been mistakenly taking on this male role because you have not read the Red Flag Man blog, and you now find yourself in a lop-sided relationship where your guy is becoming lazy and complacent, basically taking you for granted, **THEN IT'S TIME TO MAKE A BIG CHANGE!**

If he is showing less affection and attention towards you, it is not too late to re- calibrate the relationship and get it onto the right tract.

You just need determination and motivation to do so.

Your job is *not* to keep showing him how much you care and how interested in him you are or how committed to this relationship you are.
If you do make the mistake of doing these things you will see that he will pull back.
 He will be way less inclined to get together, will not spend money or time ie: (invest) in the relationship, and he will ultimately find you boring and will move on!

Why?

Because men are wired from time immemorial to go after what they want and what they want is a CHALLENGE!

They only value what they have had to work to achieve or to get.

Women who put too much work into a romantic relationship are BORING to a man. It is perceived as your pursuit of him. If you are pursuing him, why does he have to strive to impress you?
He already won you over through no effort of his own!
Now that he has you... where's the excitement?
Where is the challenge a man craves?

Our ancestral forefathers had to go out and hunt and gather in order to sustain themselves and their families. It is in their nature to love the "hunt" and the challenge of working to get the woman they are attracted to.
If you take away the need for this pursuit, you become dull and uninteresting to your man.

So how do you let him know you care?

By accepting many (but not all) of his invitations, by reciprocating affection, by making eye contact and smiling and being happy to see him.

Show appreciation when he does something big or small for you.
Just don't overdo it!

You should cultivate a sense of entitlement to his efforts to please you because you are an amazing fun person with a full and interesting life that any man would be lucky to have.

Don't really believe that about yourself?

FAKE IT TILL YOU MAKE IT!

Real Life Situation:
Lately I have been receiving emails from women wondering what they can do to get a guy they have set their sights on.

You can't make him love you by trying to convince him how great you are.

I have an email from a woman who feels that the man she likes would be way better off with her, than with his current girlfriend and she wants my advice on how to get him to realize that. She intends to fight for him and to point out to him that his girlfriend is nowhere near as good for him as she is. She has a whole list of reasons why this is so.

No man will break it off with his GF and choose you instead because you have pointed out to him all the ways you think you are better for him than she is. (Even if you are prettier or "better" than his GF.)

If he wanted to go out with you he would have chased you until he got you!

It is a terrible idea to attempt to convince a guy that you are better for him than his girlfriend because his automatic and natural response will be to defend her and to become disgusted by you.

Much like cave man days, he will protect his cave and its inhabitants.

I have emails from women who have fallen for their own male friends, with whom they now want more than a platonic relationship.

How can they get the guy to want more too?

Some of them have been having "friend sex" and wonder how to get out of the Friend Zone and into a romance.

Is that possible?

NO!

Once you have handed over the goodies to a guy, without making him earn your love and your body, its game over. Why would he chase after and value something that was just given to him without him having to make any effort at all to woo and win her?

Others are wondering how to let a particular man know that they like him and would like him to ask them out.
Well, the most you can do in this case is to smile and flirt a bit when you see him, but that's it!

The answer to all such questions is, *you can't get a guy to love you (or want you).*

If a man knows you, sees you around, has hung out with you, and yet has chosen *another* woman for a partner, or if a man has been your platonic friend and has been content in that role, or if you have made the dreadful mistake of sleeping with him as "just friends", then there is absolutely nothing that you can do to reverse that role.

Love and attraction are not logical. You cannot talk him into loving or wanting you.

No man will suddenly desire you sexually after you have been hanging out as platonic friends for a long time, and NO guy will suddenly decide that the casual sex buddy should be his GF. And the reason for all of the above is the same reason that I have been stressing to you here and in my Red Flag Man Blogs.

Men only value what they must work to have and will only desire what they must strive to achieve.

Cheap and easy is not appealing.

The allure is in the hunt and in the chase. The sexy thrill is in the capture after the struggle to win her over.

If you take away the struggle, the hunt and the chase, then it's Game Over.

If you still don't believe me, then try it your way and let me know what happens.

Chapter Twenty-Six

CLOSURE – Is It Real?

Often we find ourselves unable to move on emotionally after our romance has ended, even when a significant amount of time has gone by, because we are longing for the one missing element that we believe will empower us to do so.

We believe we need closure.

If we have experienced a toxic relationship with an abusive or personality disordered man, or if we have been cheated on, lied to, or whatever the fatal issue was, we still may find it very hard to let go emotionally.

We may tell ourselves that we could do so, *if only we had "closure"*.

But really, what does that mean?

What it means is that we are still waiting for something from the very person who failed to give us what we needed in the first place!

The relationship ended because we discovered betrayal.
We discovered dishonesty.
We experienced emotional or physical abuse.
Perhaps we discovered that he is married!
He was never available in the first place!

So we end the relationship, on some level.

We stop seeing him but we don't stop obsessing over the details of the story, analyzing it a hundred times and playing it out in our minds over and over again with every conceivable different outcome, like a script not yet written.

What we must realize is that we do not need anything from an individual who has wronged us.

If the issues that arose were powerful enough to break us apart then we must realize that the issues themselves are the root of the break up.

We must use our painful experience to move on emotionally towards a happy healthy new relationship.

Putting ourselves in the position of waiting for *anything* from Mr. Wrong is an unhealthy and impractical solution to an unsolvable problem.

We must empower ourselves, and not Mr. Wrong.
Waiting for an explanation, apology, or excuse from him just *weakens us all the more, while assigning him power over us.*

Instead, please realize that YOU are the prize and he has just lost it!

Hit the gym, hang out with your friends, write out your thoughts and feelings in a diary and stay far away from any thought of texting, calling or "bumping into" him in search for answers to questions which, if we are really honest with ourselves, are self explanatory.

How do we recognize our Mr. Right?

Great relationships are *not built* with unhealthy, unmotivated, selfish men. The man who is your own MR. RIGHT is the man who will do *whatever he has to do to be with you.*

He is into you.

He is crazy about you.

His life is not worth living without you.

He does the chasing.

He tries to win *you* over.

He overcomes any obstacle to be with you.

He beams with pride and happiness when he is with you.

He brags about your great qualities!!

His life is devoted to making you happy!

He is able and willing to be a provider.

DON'T SETTLE FOR LESS

Always remember, you deserve love. You deserve the best of everything in life.

Now go out there and get the best of everything girl!

Red Flag Man – Sources of Inspiration

Understanding Personality Disorders: An Introduction
By Dr. Duane Dobbert

Men Who Hate Women and The Women Who Love Them
By Dr. Susan Forward

Necessary Losses: The Loves, Illusions, Dependencies and Impossible
Expectations that All of Us Have to Give Up in Order to Grow
By Judith Viorst

The Road Less Traveled – A New Psychology of Love, Traditional Values and
Spiritual Growth
By M. Scott Peck MD

Hold Me Tight: Seven Conversations for a Lifetime of Love
By Dr. Sue Johnson

Ignore the Guy, Get the Guy- The Art of No Contact: A women's Survival
Guide to Mastering a Break Up and Taking Back her Power
By Leslie Braswell

Psych Central.com

Made in the USA
Middletown, DE
16 January 2023